GAMES LANGUAGE PEOPLE PLAY

JERRY STEINBERG

Dominie Press
Pippin Publishing Limited

ISBN 0-88751-017-5

First published 1983
Reprinted 1986, 1988
Second Edition 1991

Published by

Dominie Press
Pippin Publishing Limited
150 Telson Drive,
Markham, Ontario, L3R 1E5

Printed in Canada by Alger Press

TABLE OF CONTENTS

TABLE OF CONTENTS

DEDICATION

I dedicate this book of games to Bill, a former student of mine, who once confessed, "Every time we sang a song, listened to one of your corny jokes, or played a game (all in the target language, of course), we thought we were just fooling around and not working. Then, I realized that everyone was paying attention and participating, and that as much learning was taking place during the fun times as did during the formal lesson. We were laughing <u>and</u> learning. You tricked us!"

You're right, Bill. I did trick you. And in doing so, I made learning more fun for you, and teaching more fun for me.

ACKNOWLEDGEMENT

I would like to thank Sharon Ginsberg for her perceptive comments from a fresh perspective.

GAME ESSENTIALS

Things I look for in games to play with my students.

(1) Ease of Explanation: The rules of a game should be few and simple. If you are fortunate enough to be able to speak the background (native) language(s) of all of your students, I would suggest taking a few minutes to explain the game in that/those language(s) and use the remaining time to play the game. (I would rather spend a few minutes explaining the game and have lots of time left over to play it, than use up all the time explaining it in the target language and have no time left to play.)

If you cannot communicate with students in their own language(s), use the simplest vocabulary possible, utilizing lots of visual aids and giving lots of concrete examples, to ensure comprehension.

(2) Absence of expensive or complicated materials.

(3) Versatility: I like games that can easily be adapted to suit the number, age, and linguistic level of my students.

LINGUISTIC SKILLS

Under each game title, I have indicated which linguistic skills are involved in playing the game. They are **L**istening, **S**peaking, **R**eading and **W**riting. Letters in parentheses indicate the linguistic skills which can be practised if the game is adapted.

Feel free to modify the games to emphasize or de-emphasize any particular linguistic skills – I often do!

EXAMPLES

Examples given in this book are exactly that – samples, models, guides to be followed, modified, and expanded to suit your needs. They are not intended to be used exactly as they appear, nor are they meant to represent all possibilities.

LEVEL

I have attempted to indicate which level of learner (Beginner, Intermediate, or Advanced) each game is best suited to, but please keep in mind that the meaning of each term will vary according to the educational situation of the individual teacher. So please examine each game with the intention of adapting it to suit your students.

REFERENCE TO PERSONS

The generic HE, HIS, and HIM have been employed to increase ease of reading and economy of space. No discrimination is intended.

OPTIMAL GROUP SIZE

During my demonstrations of linguistic games for the language classroom, teachers have often expressed the concern that it is next to impossible to play games with classes of 30 to 40 (or more) students.

Although some games are well-suited to large groups (YES/NO PING-PONG, LETTERGORY and WHAT'S NEW?, to name a few), to ensure total involvement and participation of all students, teams of no more than 10 students are recommended. This enables each and every student to take an active part in the game and to contribute to his team's effort, in addition to permitting the teacher to monitor each individual's performance.

So, what should you do if you have upwards of 30 students in your class? Send half of them home? No! I suggest "Activity Stations."

Divide your class into equal teams (as nearly as possible) and assign each group to an Activity Station. By way of illustration, a class of 40 could have 4 teams of 10 students each. Team A could go to Station One, where they could, for example, listen to a taped story and answer written questions about the story. Team B, at Station Two, could do crossword puzzles. Team C would play T.V. DEFINITION (or another suitable game) against Team D under the direction of the teacher at Station Three.

After a given length of time (for example, 15 minutes), the groups would move on to the next station in a clockwise direction: Team A would advance to Station Two, B to Three, and D to One, leaving Team C at Station Three to compete against Team B. This rotation could take place the next day, depending on your schedule. This takes a bit of organization, but once the system is learned, it functions quite smoothly, and students move from one station to the next with a minimum of noise and confusion.

Here is how the rotation would work. Each diagram represents one session.

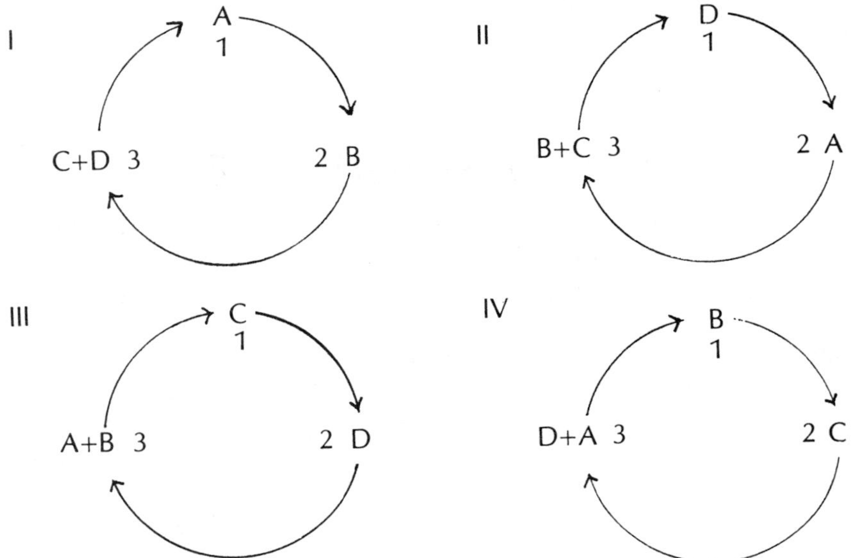

And here is a partial list of alternative activities which students at Stations One and Two could engage in while waiting to play at Station Three. (All are to be done in the target language, of course.)

- Reading comic books;
- Listening to a taped song and doing a cloze exercise;
- Watching a video-taped program and answering written questions;
- Creating a dialogue or skit on a given theme;
- Reading a story and answering written questions;
- Doing written exercises on grammar or vocabulary;
- Listening to a taped dialogue and answering questions;
- Creating a story on a given theme;
- Reading a newspaper article in preparation for discussion;
- Listening to a taped newscast and answering questions;
- Doing word searches or crossword puzzles;
- Reading a dialogue and answering questions;
- Playing quiet games which don't require the teacher's presence or supervision.

WHEN TO PLAY GAMES

Games can be played at any time. I frequently play a short game with my students at the beginning of the lesson, especially on Mondays, to welcome them back, refresh their memories, and warm them up for learning new material. You know only too well how much can be forgotten over the weekend, and how difficult it is to "get their motors started," particularly on Mondays. What better way to review last week's (or yesterday's) learning than by playing a game which requires students to recall and use that information repeatedly?

Also, occasionally, I will interrupt a lesson to play a short, snappy game when I find students' attention waning. I then return to the lesson with alert and attentive students.

Saving a game for the end of the session also has its advantages. It will encourage students to co-operate during the lesson and, by ending on a "high note," it may entice them to return for the next session.

In summary, the best time to play a game is <u>any time</u> that a game will benefit your students.

THE PEDAGOGICAL VALUE OF GAMES

Everyone knows that games are fun, but some people think that they are *only fun* — lacking any pedagogical value. Not so! Games are a viable (and enjoyable) method of achieving many educational and behavioural objectives. For example:

I use games to **reinforce** newly acquired information, immediately after it has been taught.

Days, weeks, months, even years after something has been taught, a game is a delightful way to **review** that material.

A game makes an excellent **reward** to encourage students to co-operate (or to thank them for co-operating) during less enjoyable activities.

After a gruelling oral drill, or other energy-draining exercise, a quiet game is a fun way to **relax**.

Games tend to **reduce inhibition,** especially if the competitive element is diminished or eliminated. The shy or linguistically weak student will feel more at ease and will participate more freely, if the object is just to have fun, and not to score points and win. Although competition often adds excitement and increases participation, it also intensifies the pressure to perform well, thereby excluding the timid student and the one who is less sure of his facility with the language.

No matter how dynamic a teacher you are, there are bound to be occasional general lapses in attention. A short, snappy game will **raise attentiveness,** revive the class, and make them more receptive to further learning.

A game provides the teacher with a method of **rapid rectification** of students' errors. Correcting errors immediately prevents them from becoming deeply rooted in students' memories.

Students tend to remember best the things they enjoyed doing. Hence, games **aid retention.**

Playing games takes the drudgery out of learning and, thus, **provides motivation.**

Students are very co-operative during games, since no one wants to risk being responsible for bringing a pleasurable activity to a premature end. Consequently, games help to **restrain rebellion.**

1. T.V. DEFINITION

L, S, R

levels: all
optimal group size: 10
(For larger groups, see ADAPTATION.)

OBJECTIVE: For Advanced classes, to introduce or review idiomatic expressions. For Beginners and Intermediate classes, to review vocabulary and spelling.

MATERIALS NEEDED: Blackboard or overhead projector, and several T.V. DEFINITIONS.

DESCRIPTION: The group is divided into 5 teams of 2 players each. In turn, one player from each team will GIVE AWAY a letter of the alphabet he hopes **isn't** in the solution. If that letter indeed isn't in the solution, his partner will TAKE a letter he hopes **is** in the solution. If it is, the correctly TAKEN letter is written into its place(s) in the solution, and that team can guess at the solution. If a letter is GIVEN AWAY and **is** in the solution, that team loses its turn, and the next team has a free guess at the solution in addition to their regular turn to GIVE AWAY and TAKE letters.

If the TAKEN letter **isn't** in the solution, that team loses its chance to guess at the solution. For example:

DEFINITION: *What students are when they fall asleep in class.*

SOLUTION: _ _ _ _ _   _ _   _ _ _ _ _ _ _ _ _ _

(Each dash represents a letter of the solution.)

The group is broken up into teams A,B,C,D, and E. Player A1 is asked to GIVE AWAY a letter he hopes **isn't** in the solution. He GIVES AWAY "Z." There is no "Z" in the solution, so player A2 can now TAKE a letter he hopes **is** in the solution. He takes "E." There are 2 "Es" in the solution and they are written into their spaces:

_ _ _ **E** _   _ _   **E** _ _ _ _ _ _ _ _

Team A, having GIVEN AWAY and TAKEN correctly, can now guess at the solution, but it's really too early in the game to have much of a chance of guessing correctly. So, Team A passes.

B1 GIVES AWAY "Q." There are no "Qs" in the solution, so player B2 TAKES "O." There are 3 "Os" in the solution, and they are now written into their spaces:

_ **O** _ E _   **O** _   E _ _ _ _ _ _ **O** _

Team B passes on their guess since there still isn't enough information to help them make a correct guess.

Player C1 GIVES AWAY "B," but there **is** a "B" in the solution. The "B" is written into its space and Team C loses its chance to guess. Team D then gets a free guess.

B O _ E _   O _   E _ _ _ _ _ _ O _

They decide to pass, since they aren't really sure of the solution, and they take their regular turn at GIVING AWAY and TAKING letters.

Player D1 GIVES AWAY "X" correctly, and D2 TAKES "M." As there are no "Ms" in the solution, Team D loses its chance to guess.

Player E1 GIVES AWAY "J" correctly, and E2 TAKES "U" correctly. All "Us" are written in (there's only one):

B O _ E _   O _   E _ **U** _ _ _ _ O _

Team E takes a wild guess at the solution, but is wrong. Player A1 now GIVES AWAY "R" by mistake. There **is** an "R" in the solution, and after it is written in, Team B has a free guess:

B O **R** E _   O _   E _ U _ _ _ _ O _

They guess "BORED OF EDUCATION" and win the match since that is the solution to *What students are when they fall asleep in class.*

Here are some other T.V. DEFINITIONS that I have used with my students:

A Russian garden	A COMMUNIST PLOT
Refusing to sleep	RESISTING A REST
Afraid to eat at Colonel Sanders'	CHICKENING OUT
Alimony	THE HIGH COST OF LEAVING
Drink for a small person	SHRIMP COCKTAIL
What sleepy drivers do	THEY REST IN PIECES

ADAPTATION: When an entire class is involved, teams could consist of 5 to 7 players each, instead of 2 as outlined in the example.

Note: This game is an adaptation of the television game Definition. Hence the name T.V. DEFINITION.

SUGGESTIONS: I write the alphabet beneath the solution dashes and erase each letter as it is GIVEN AWAY and TAKEN. That way, it is GIVEN AWAY and TAKEN only once.

For Beginners and Intermediate groups, instead of using puns of idiomatic expressions, I simply challenge them with:

It's an animal: _ _ _ _ _ _ _ _ _

or

It's a language: _ _ _ _ _ _ _ _ _ _

To help students be more successful in the game, I suggest that they GIVE AWAY letters which are not frequently used, such as X, Q, Z, and J; and to TAKE vowels first, since every word must contain at least 1 vowel.

They are encouraged to confer with their partners as to which letter to GIVE AWAY or TAKE, and, of course, when they guess at the solution.

2. TIC-TAC-VOCAB

L, S

levels: all
optimal group size: 20

OBJECTIVE: To review and reinforce the use of vocabulary items (for Beginning classes) or to strengthen the ability to define words (for Intermediate and Advanced groups).

MATERIALS NEEDED: Overhead projector, one acetate with a large TIC-TAC-TOE grid on it.

1	2	3
4	5	6
7	8	9

Many (20 plus) pictures of known vocabulary items (nouns and verbs) drawn on pieces of clear acetate (small enough to fit into the 9 positions on the grid, about 2″ by 3″ or 5 cm by 8 cm) and 9 each of X and O on acetate pieces of the same size.

DESCRIPTION: A drawing is placed in each of the 9 positions of the grid. The group (of 20) is divided into 2 teams (Team X and Team O).

The first player chooses a position on the grid and names the word occupying that space, for example: "Number 1. It's an apple." If correct, he puts his team's symbol (X or O) into that space. A player on the other team now tries to identify a word in any vacant position which will help his team occupy 3 positions in a row – vertically, horizontally, or diagonally. If a mistake is made, the position remains vacant until the word in it is correctly identified.

The first team to occupy 3 positions in a row wins.

Sample grid:

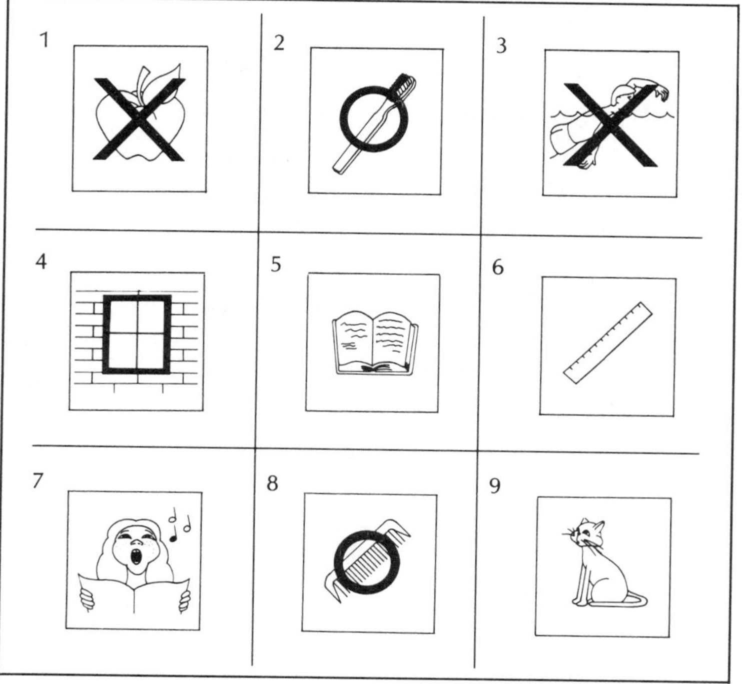

ADAPTATION: For Intermediate and Advanced classes, simply identifying the word isn't enough. You have to name it and define it (size, colour, shape, material, where it is found, how it is used, where it is done, etc). For example:

> "A *toothbrush* is an instrument, usually made of plastic, with a handle about five inches long (13 cm), with bristles on one end, used with toothpaste to clean the teeth."
>
> "*Swim* is an action performed in water to propel oneself."

3. GUIDE WORD

L, S, R, W

levels: all
optimal group size: unlimited

OBJECTIVE: To reinforce students' appreciation of the composition and spelling of words.

MATERIALS NEEDED: Pencils, dictionaries, and copies of the GUIDE WORD challenge.

DESCRIPTION: The teacher assigns a random number to each letter of the alphabet. The GUIDE WORD is given with the corresponding numbers below the letters. For example:

G	U	I	D	E
23	10	19	16	8

Then several coded words are presented and the students are challenged to decipher the codes. For example:

$\overline{\ }$ 9 $\overline{\ }$ 12 $\overline{\ }$ 5 $\overline{\ }$ 3 $\overline{\ }$ 8 $\overline{\ }$ 14

$\overline{\ }$ 16 $\overline{\ }$ 8 $\overline{\ }$ 5 $\overline{\ }$ 7

$\overline{\ }$ 6 $\overline{\ }$ 9 $\overline{\ }$ 10 $\overline{\ }$ 23 $\overline{\ }$ 1

SUGGESTIONS: Students could work in teams (of 2 or 3) to facilitate and expedite the decoding. Assigning numbers to letters is easiest when the letters are printed in order and numbers are assigned randomly (from 1 to 26). For example:

A	B	C	D	E	. . . .	Z
9	20	4	16	8		13

After each letter has been assigned a number, present 15 to 20 coded words (showing numbers only) to the students for decoding. The first student (or team) to decode the entire list is the winner.

4. FOUR-SQUARE

L, R, W

levels: all
optimal group size: unlimited

OBJECTIVE: To develop vocabulary and improve spelling ability.

MATERIALS NEEDED: Dictionary, pen and paper for each student.

DESCRIPTION: Each student draws a grid 4 spaces by 4 spaces on his paper. The teacher calls out 16 random letters and the students place those letters in the spaces on their grids, in any arrangement. Students are then challenged to make words from adjoining letters.

Rules: Only adjoining letters may be used to make a word and each letter can be used only once per word.
Time limit: 3 minutes.

Example:

C	E	I	K
H	S	R	A
O	E	P	B
M	N	L	O

BAR
PAR
PAIR
PARE
ARE
ARK
ARIES
HELP
PERSON

BARS
RISE
RAISE
CHOSE
CHOSEN
HOME
HOMES
SHOE
PARK

SUGGESTIONS: I always make sure that there are at least 5 vowels called out. Since every word must contain at least 1 vowel, students would be severely restricted if fewer than 5 of the 16 letters were vowels. Also, to encourage my students to look for "million dollar words" (that is, longer words), I award bonus points for longer words. Two- to four-letter words are worth 1 point each; five-letter words earn 2 points each; six-letter words gain 3 points each, and so on. With Advanced groups, I do not accept words comprising fewer than 4 letters.

Note: If you are familiar with the commercial game Boggle, FOUR-SQUARE is quite similar. You could call it Poor Man's Boggle, since it costs nothing to play.

5. TIC-TAC-VERB

L, S, R

levels: all
optimal group size: 20

OBJECTIVE: To review a particular verb tense.

MATERIALS NEEDED: Overhead projector, blackboard, or self-made board (see SUGGESTIONS).

DESCRIPTION: A verb is placed into each of the 9 positions on the grid. For example:

eat	speak	swim
watch	run	laugh
write	walk	drink

The verb tense to be reviewed is demonstrated, for example, Present Continuous/Progressive – "The baby is sleeping now." The group is divided into 2 teams (namely, Team X and Team O). A volunteer from Team X chooses a position on the grid and names the verb in that position. For example: "I choose 'eat.' " He then uses that verb in a suitable sentence, using the chosen tense, for example, "John is eating breakfast." If he is correct, an X is placed in that position, indicating that Team X now occupies that position. If he makes an error, one that could lead to misunderstanding, the position is left vacant, and Team O can now try for any vacant position which will help them occupy 3 positions in a row (vertically, horizontally, or diagonally).

When one team wins, verbs which have been used are replaced by new ones, and a new round is begun by the losing team.

ADAPTATION: I often use the following symbols over the verbs to direct students to use the interrogative [?], affirmative [✓] or [+], and negative [X] or [—].

SUGGESTIONS: I don't accept terse statements (such as, "John is eating.") since they don't indicate that the meaning of the verb is clear to the student, and they show little creativity. I ask the student to expand such short sentences.

Also, I have found that students prefer games which have some concrete materials, partly because it shows greater interest and preparation on the part of the teacher, and because they enjoy handling the materials. So, if you can find the time, you could make a TIC-TAC-TOE board and use curtain hooks to support the verb cards (and the X and O overlays) in their positions. If you can't, at least allow each student to mark his X or his O on the grid over his verb (whether on the blackboard or on the overhead projector). This gives them a greater feeling of involvement and gets them up and out of their seats for a moment.

Tic-Tac-Toe board:

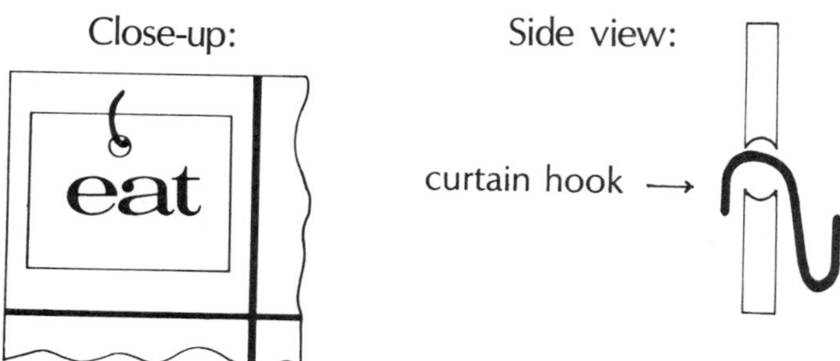

6. DICTIONARY

L, S

levels: all
optimal group size: unlimited

OBJECTIVE: To develop critical listening skills and comprehension of definitions.

MATERIALS NEEDED: Provide a dictionary geared to the linguistic capabilities of your students; preferably one which, in addition to defining words, shows the word in context. One that I have found quite suitable for most ESL classes is the *New Horizon Ladder Dictionary of the English Language*, New American Library, New York, 1970. Almost any dictionary will do, and, in a pinch, the teacher can make up definitions for each word.

DESCRIPTION: The teacher finds a suitable word in the dictionary, names the part of speech (noun, verb, etc.) and the first letter, and reads the definitions (and the sentences using the word in context, if necessary). The students try to guess the word being defined. The first student correctly to identify the word chooses the next word and reads its definitions. For example:

> "My word is a verb and it begins with the letter 't'. It means: 1. produce thoughts; form in the mind. *I often ______ of home.* 2. reason; consider. *He is ______ about the problem.* 3. believe; have faith in something. *He ______ he can do it."*

SUGGESTION: For classes that tend to get over-excited, I divide them into 2 teams, subtract 2 points for each wrong guess and add 5 for a correct guess. This encourages students to listen carefully and to think, instead of calling out every word they know that begins with the named letter.

7. QUESTION BASEBALL

L, S, R

levels: all
optimal group size: 20

OBJECTIVE: To assess and increase students' knowledge of grammar, mathematics, and general information.

MATERIALS NEEDED: Four lists of questions of varying difficulty are presented, each list being more advanced than the last. Questions can deal with grammar, mathematics, and general information. There should be at least 10 questions per list.

DESCRIPTION: Three bases and home plate are indicated in the room. They may be marked on the floor or be represented by specially designated desks.

The group is divided into 2 teams of 10 players each. One team pitches (asks the questions) while the other is at bat (answers the questions).

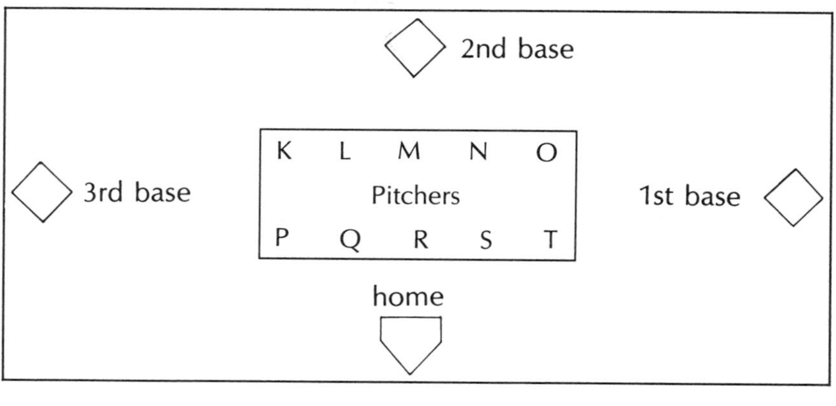

Batters can choose from among Single Hit (very easy) questions, Double Hit (slightly harder) questions, Triple Hit (harder still) questions, and Home Run (the most difficult) questions. When a batter answers the chosen question correctly, he advances that number of bases. All batters ahead of him advance that number of bases.

Each time a batter crosses home plate, a point is scored. If a batter doesn't know the answer, or answers incorrectly, he is out (no 3 strikes in this version). When three batters are out, the teams exchange roles.

Note: The beauty of this game is that, due to the range of difficulty and complexity of the questions, students of *all* abilities can be active contributors to their teams' progress.

Here is a sample progression:

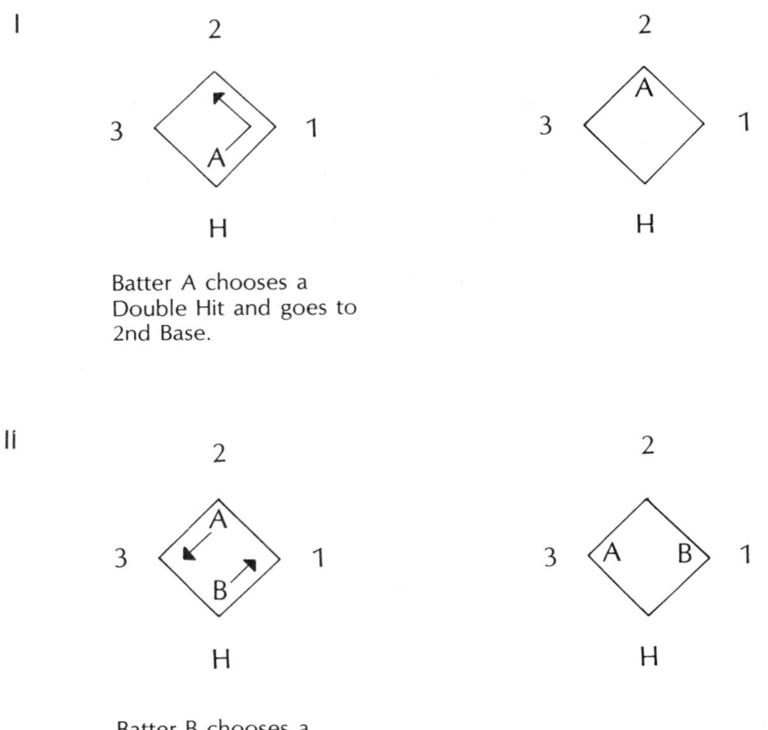

III

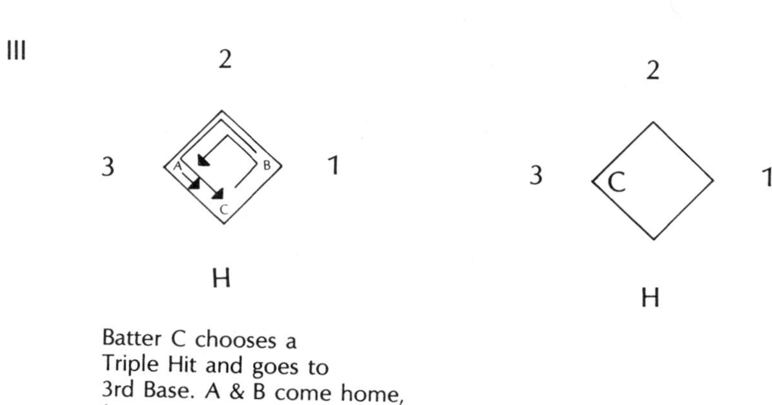

Batter C chooses a Triple Hit and goes to 3rd Base. A & B come home, for 2 points.

IV

Batter D chooses a Single Hit and goes to 1st Base, while C comes home (1 point).

V

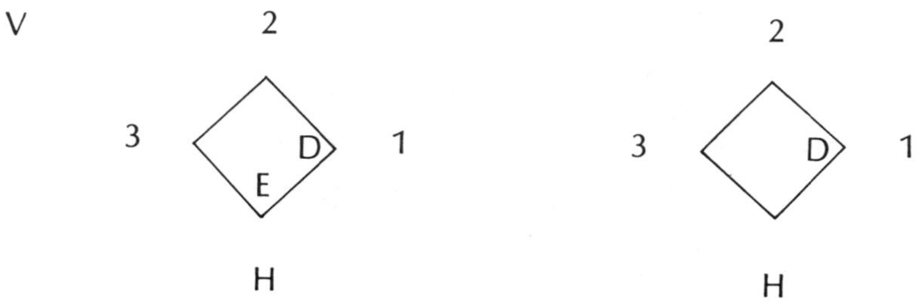

Batter E chooses a Home Run, but answers incorrectly, and is struck out.

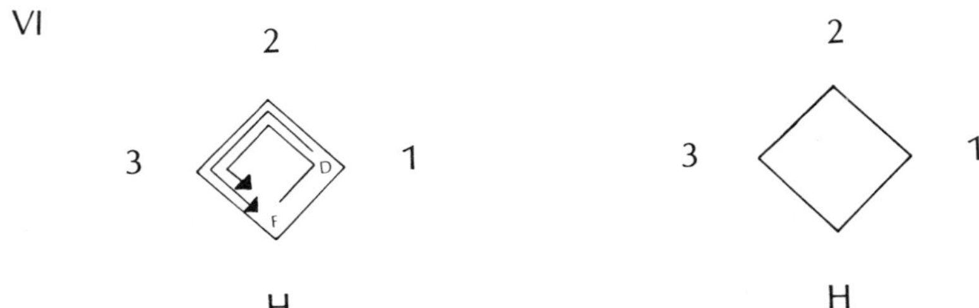

Batter F chooses a Home Run, is correct, and both D and F come home for 2 more points.

In example IV above, Batter D causes C to come home and score a point by correctly answering a simple question.

Here are some possible sample questions. You would tailor them to suit the knowledge and abilities of your students.

Single Hit: What is your name?
Name the two official languages of Canada.
How old are you?
What is the plural of "he"?
How much is six plus four?

Double Hit: Where do you live?
How much does a dozen eggs cost?
What is the population of Canada?
Change to "she": *I watch television.*
How much is ninety minus sixty-two?

Triple Hit: Who was the previous prime minister of Canada?
Name the capital cities of Manitoba and Newfoundland.
Change to past: *I see the bird.*
How much is six times eight?
Spell "dictionary".

Home Run: Name four teams of the CFL, city and name.
Who was the prime minister of Canada in 1962?
Change to past continuous: *Shirley looked out the window.*
How much is nine times seven, minus twenty-four?

SUGGESTION: You might want to limit the time allowed to formulate and deliver a response to each question.

8. TRIPLE DEFINITIONS

L, R, W

levels: all
optimal group size: unlimited

OBJECTIVE: To refine listening skills and improve students' ability to recognize vocabulary items.

MATERIALS NEEDED: Paper and pencil for each student. A list of 30 or more suitable words on the blackboard or overhead.

DESCRIPTION: Each student draws an X and O grid on a piece of paper, and chooses 9 words from the master list of 30 or more words which are on the blackboard (or overhead). He writes his 9 words into the 9 squares on his grid. For example, one student might choose the following 9 words and place them in this arrangement.

eat	~~small~~	carrot
music	socks	~~laugh~~
~~knife~~	sleep	~~hungry~~

The teacher now chooses words randomly from the master list and, instead of naming the words, gives a definition of each. For example:

It's the opposite of "big."
What you do when someone tells a funny joke.
What you use to cut meat.
How you feel when you haven't eaten in a long time.

When a word on his grid matches the definition given by the teacher, the student crosses it out. The first person to have 3 words crossed out in a row (vertically, horizontally, or diagonally) is the winner. New grids are made and filled in with new words and a new round is begun.

ADAPTATIONS: This game could also be played mathematically. For example:

25	~~37~~	24
20	29	47
42	43	~~35~~

(Numbers are from 20 to 50.)

The teacher says: The answer is 20 plus 17.
The answer is 5 times 7.

Another idea is to have the numbers spelled out in the spaces instead of using the numerals.

~~fourteen~~	twenty-six	seventeen
twenty-one	~~twelve~~	~~thirty-three~~
thirty-eight	nineteen	eleven

SUGGESTIONS: I tell my students that the definitions will be given **only once**. This makes them listen more attentively.

Also, to ensure that the winner has indeed won, I ask him to read the words (or numbers) that gave him the win.

9. HIDDEN SENTENCE

R, W

levels: all
optimal group size: unlimited

OBJECTIVE: To improve students' appreciation of syntax and spelling.

MATERIALS NEEDED: Overhead projector, blackboard, or copies of the following grids on paper.

DESCRIPTION: Depending on the abilities of the students, choose a square 3 X 3 spaces, 4 X 4, 5 X 5, etc, and fill the spaces with the letters of a predetermined sentence. You can go in any direction, *except diagonally.* The sentence should have exactly the same number of letters as there are spaces in the square; that is, 9 (for a 3 × 3), 16 (for a 4 × 4), 25 (for a 5 × 5), 36 (for a 6 × 6) etc. Each letter can be used only once. Examples:

3 X 3 grid.

9 letters total.
Arrows are to aid you.

SUE TOOK IT.

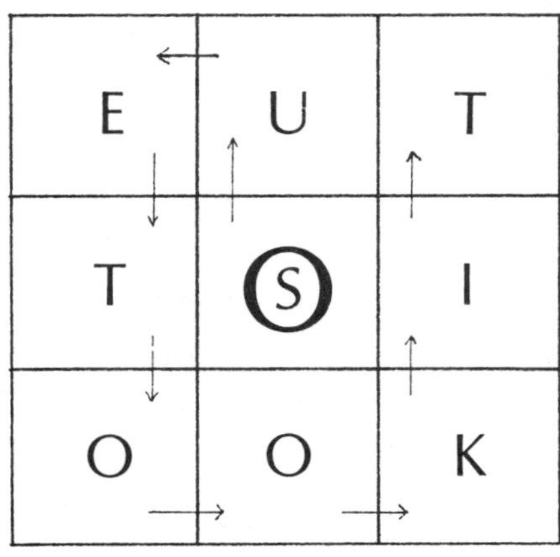

5 × 5 grid.
25 letters total.
Arrows are to aid you.

WE ATE POPCORN DURING THE SHOW.

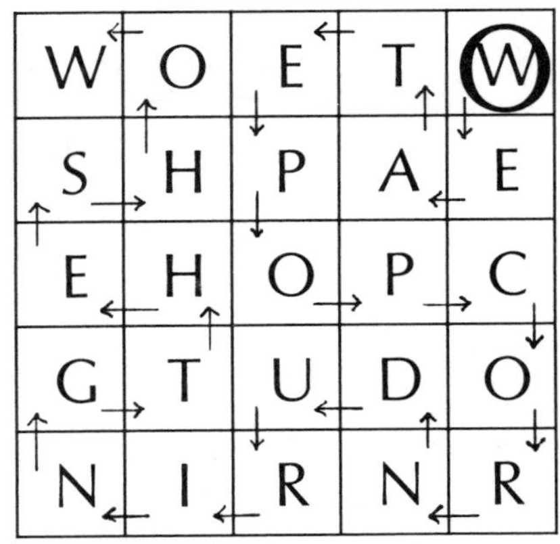

Challenge the entire class to discover the HIDDEN SENTENCE.

After half the class has discovered the solution, show, or have a student show, the solution to the others. Give them another challenge, this time, a little more difficult. Once most of the group have solved the problem, have one student show it to the rest of the group. Now, they are ready to create their own HIDDEN SENTENCES and challenge one another.

SUGGESTIONS: I find it best to start with a simple game, like having a sentence with no spaces between the words. The class is challenged to break up the sentence into words. For example: HEWILLNEVERFORGETHER. Then, a sentence in which the words are jumbled and must be re-arranged to form a correct sentence: WILL HER HE FORGET NEVER.

Next, scrambled words in jumbled order:
VENRE ERH EH LIWL FOTGER

Now, they are ready (or should be) to work with HIDDEN SENTENCES in squares. I usually use a 3 X 3 to introduce the game for the first time. Then a 4 X 4 to challenge them.

It is recommended to have the first letter of the sentence circled to facilitate solution. For more difficult challenges, perhaps the letters of the first word should be circled.

The easiest way to create a HIDDEN SENTENCE is to write down a sentence within the students' ability, such as: HE WILL NEVER FORGET HER, and add or subtract letters to make it 9, 16, 25, 36, 49, 64, 81 or 100 letters long. So, in the example which is 20 letters long, one could subtract 4 letters, or add 5. Hence, we could start with the sentence HE NEVER FORGOT HER which has 16 letters (4 × 4), or the sentence HE WILL NEVER FORGET HER SMILE which has 25 letters (5 × 5).

10. PASSWORD

L, S, R

levels: all
optimal group size: 10
(For larger groups, see ADAPTATIONS.)

OBJECTIVE: To develop vocabulary.

MATERIALS NEEDED: Small slips of paper with one word on each. These can be nouns, verbs, adjectives, adverbs, or prepositions that are familiar to the students.

DESCRIPTION: Students are divided into 5 teams of 2. For groups larger than 10, see ADAPTATIONS. One partner (A1, B1, C1, D1 and E1) of each team is shown the PASSWORD (for example, CUP), and in turn, says ***one word***, which will, he hopes, prompt his partner to say the PASSWORD. A1 might say "glass" which might prompt his partner, A2, to guess "window". B1 could give "drink" as his clue, and B2 might respond with "milk". C1 could try "coffee", while his partner, C2, might be tempted to answer "tea." D1 could use "saucer" as his clue, and that might encourage D2 to reply "cup." That being the PASSWORD, team D wins one point. Now, the other partner of each team (#2) would be shown the next PASSWORD, and D2, the last winner, would begin the next round. The starting position is the most difficult, thus winning has its drawbacks since the winner has to start the next round.

ADAPTATIONS: If you cannot break your class up into groups of 10 students, there are at least 2 ways in which this game can be adapted to suit large groups.

First, you could divide the group into any number of equal (as nearly as possible) teams. For example, a class of 37 students could be broken up into 5 teams of 5 students each and 2 teams of 6. Hence:

Team A	Team B	Team C	Team D	Team E	Team F	Team G
A1	B1	C1	D1	E1	F1	G1
A2	B2	C2	D2	E2	F2	G2
A3	B3	C3	D3	E3	F3	G3
A4	B4	C4	D4	E4	F4	G4
A5	B5	C5	D5	E5	F5	G5
					F6	G6

The first person on each team is shown the PASSWORD and when his turn comes up, he says one word to the next person (#2) on his team who tries to guess the PASSWORD. The next time his turn comes up, he would give his clue to the next in line (#3). When the PASSWORD is discovered, the #2 person on each team is shown the next PASSWORD and takes his turn giving clues to his team members in turn.

Alternatively, one person could come up to the front of the room and be shown the PASSWORD. He would then give one clue to the class and choose a person to respond to that clue. The value of the responses diminishes with successive clues. For example, if the PASSWORD is guessed on the first clue, the person at the front wins 10 points. If the second clue is the one that claims the PASSWORD, nine points would be won, and so on, until no points are left. That means that a person has a maximum of 10 clues to give for each PASSWORD.

SUGGESTIONS: I encourage my students to build upon previous clues by using hints such as "opposite" or "longer" or "similar" as their clue. Also, giving the part of speech (noun, for example) as a clue helps others to zero in on the PASSWORD.

I allow my students to use dictionaries and thesauruses, but not while it is their turn to speak. This eliminates long waits while the speaker searches for an appropriate clue.

Clues and guesses may be repeated by others as their clues. To make the game more challenging, I stipulate that clues cannot contain or be contained within the PASSWORD. For example, if the PASSWORD is "blackboard," students may not use "black" or "board" as a clue to elicit the PASSWORD from their partners. "Pencil" can't be used as a clue for "pen" since it contains the PASSWORD.

I also disallow the use of proper nouns as clues. This prevents students from insulting one another if the PASSWORD is a word such as "ugly" or "stupid."

11. SEGMENTED SENTENCES

R, W

levels: all
optimal group size: unlimited

OBJECTIVE: To assess and strengthen students' appreciation of syntax.

MATERIALS NEEDED: Index cards (200 to 400) and felt-tip markers. The smaller (3″ by 5″, or 7.5 cm by 13 cm) index cards are fine.

DESCRIPTION: The teacher composes a number of sentences that are within the linguistic ability of the students. Each sentence is written on a separate pile of cards, one word per card, and the shuffled pile is given to a student who is challenged to place the word-cards in correct order. For example:

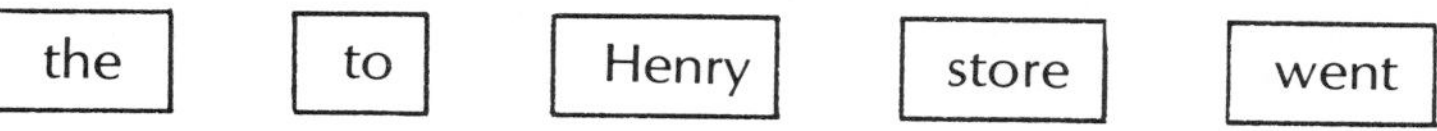

When a student feels confident that his sentence is correct, he checks it with the teacher. When the sentence is correct, he shuffles his cards and exchanges piles.

ADAPTATION: Instead of the teacher making the SEGMENTED SENTENCES, students could create them and write the words on the index cards.

SUGGESTIONS: Students could work in teams of 3 to 5. This enables them to learn from one another and reduces the number of sentences required.

To ensure that students don't have to wait between sentences there should be more sentences than the number of students (or teams) in the class.

Faster students could help check the sentences of the other students.

To prevent the cards of various sentences from getting mixed up, and students from being frustrated by missing cards, the cards could be coded to show groups and the number of cards in a group. For example:

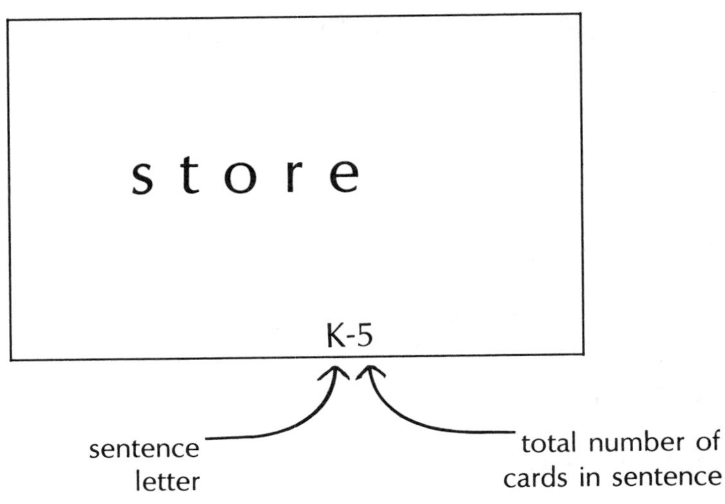

12. DIAMOND WORD

R, W

levels: all
optimal group size: unlimited

OBJECTIVE: To reinforce students' appreciation of the composition and spelling of words.

MATERIALS NEEDED: Blackboard or overhead projector, paper and pencil.

DESCRIPTION: The teacher chooses the DIAMOND WORD which comprises 4 to 8 letters, for example, HELLO. Then, words containing at least one of the letters of the DIAMOND WORD are given, in scrambled fashion (for example, PHEL). Beside each scrambled word, dashes are used to represent letters of the word (for example, PHEL __ __ __ __), and a diamond is placed on an appropriate dash to indicate that the letter in that space is in the DIAMOND WORD (for example, PHEL ◊ __ ◊ __).

Supply enough scrambled words to use all the letters of the DIAMOND WORD. For example:

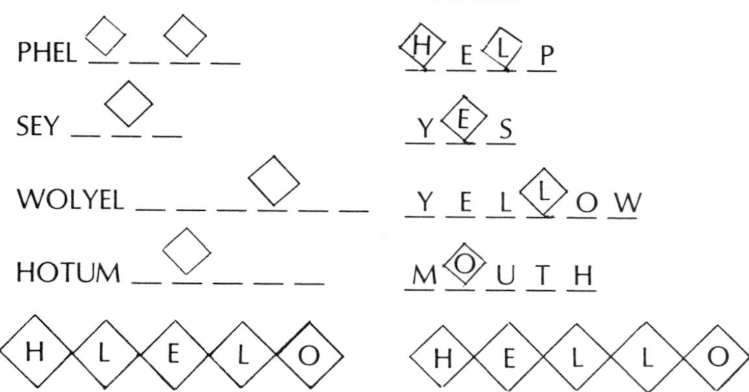

13. WORD SCRAMBLES

R, W

levels: all
optimal group size: unlimited

OBJECTIVE: To develop vocabulary and improve spelling ability.

MATERIALS NEEDED: A list of scrambled words, paper and pencils, overhead or blackboard optional.

DESCRIPTION: The students are presented a list of scrambled words on the blackboard, overhead, or paper, and are challenged to unscramble them. The first person, or team, to unscramble the entire list wins. The words, of course, are from known active and passive vocabulary. For example:

HYPAP	OAPIN
POSA	MECARA
SIFH	

The length of the list depends on the time available and the interest level of the students.

ADAPTATION: The list can occasionally be restricted to a category such as occupations, world capitals, political leaders, or furniture.

SUGGESTION: To introduce the game to students for the first time, I usually start by having teams of 3 to 5 players each compete against one another. Working in teams enables individuals to learn from one another and helps to build self-confidence.

14. DO

L, S

levels: all
optimal group size: unlimited

OBJECTIVE: To practise asking questions with DO and identifying actions in the appropriate tense (Present Continuous/Progressive, Future, Simple Past and Present Perfect.)

MATERIALS NEEDED: None.

DESCRIPTION: This game can be called:

WHAT AM I DOING?
WHAT AM I GOING TO DO?
WHAT DID I DO?
WHAT HAVE I DONE?

The choice of the title depends on the tense being reviewed.

THE PRESENT CONTINUOUS: While the action *is being performed,* the actor asks, "What am I doing?" The person who answers correctly (for example, "You are walking.") can either replace the actor, or win a point (for his team, if teams have been formed).

THE FUTURE TENSE: (going to) The actor *prepares to perform* an action and asks, "What am I going to do?" A correct response might be "You're going to sit down."

THE SIMPLE PAST TENSE: The actor, when *finished performing* an action, asks, "What did I do?" An appropriate answer could be "You drank some water."

THE PRESENT PERFECT TENSE: The actor, *after having performed* an action, asks, "What have I done?" Someone could win a point with the answer "You have written on the blackboard."

15. COMMANDS

L, S

level: beginners
optimal group size: 20

OBJECTIVE: To review the use of the imperative.

MATERIALS NEEDED: None.

DESCRIPTION: The group is divided into 2 teams (A and B). Students take turns giving a command to their opponents on the other team. One point for a correct command and 1 for the correct action. The difficulty and complexity of commands will depend on the ability of your students. Examples:

A1: "Touch your toes!"
B1: Performs the action.

B1: "Point to the window!"
A1: Performs the action.

A2: "Laugh quietly!"
B2: Performs the action.

B2: "Untie your shoe!"
A2: Performs the action.

SUGGESTIONS: Commands should, of course, be reasonable and physically possible to perform. To encourage students to be creative and original, 2 points could be awarded for novel commands, while ordinary or repeated commands are worth only 1 point.

16. TIC-TAC-NUMBER

L, S, R, W

level: beginners
optimal group size: unlimited

OBJECTIVE: To review cardinal numbers.

MATERIALS NEEDED: Pen and paper for each student.

DESCRIPTION: Students are instructed to draw a grid with 2 vertical and 2 horizontal lines (3 for a longer game). They then fill the 9 (or 16) spaces with numbers (within a prescribed range) in any order. Examples:

Short Game

(range 1 – 25)

1	~~12~~	~~8~~
14	~~20~~	13
~~21~~	25	~~6~~

Long Game

(range 1 –50)

~~6~~	34	~~9~~	50
18	~~31~~	26	~~14~~
~~27~~	45	~~2~~	40
10	~~38~~	49	~~42~~

The teacher now calls out random numbers and students cross out called numbers that appear on their grids. The first person to eliminate 3 (or 4) numbers in a row (vertically, horizontally, or diagonally) wins. To prove the validity of his claim, the winner must call out the 3 (or 4) numbers that gave him the win. The winner can call the numbers for the next round.

ADAPTATION: TIC-TAC-LETTER – Letters, instead of numbers, are placed in the spaces.

K	B	M
P	W	L
O	R	S

SUGGESTION: To avoid controversy, I encourage the use of **pens** and tell my students that they must print clearly and legibly. Any number that has been changed or tampered with will be rejected.

17. SURPRISE SACK

L, S, R, W

level: beginners
optimal group size: 20

OBJECTIVE: To give students practice in description.

MATERIALS NEEDED: Each student brings a common object, such as a comb, cup, penny, sock, etc. A bag is optional.

DESCRIPTION: Students take turns describing, in detail, the objects they have brought to class, while the others try to guess the identity of each one. For example:

> "My object is about 4 inches (10 cm) long. It weighs about 6 ounces (150 g). It is oblong in shape. It is made of nylon. It is flexible, and is dull black. What is it?"

SUGGESTIONS: Terms to describe aspects such as size, weight, shape, colour, texture, material, etc., should be familiar to students before this game is played. Students could write out their descriptions beforehand to facilitate playing the game.

I have found that students' interest is aroused when the object in question is contained in a paper bag. It seems to pique their curiosity more by **almost** being able to see the object as it is being described, than when the object is totally concealed in a desk.

18. WHERE WAS I?

L, S, R, W

level: beginners
optimal group size: unlimited

OBJECTIVE: To practise using the verb TO BE in the Simple Past (interrogative, affirmative, and negative).

MATERIALS NEEDED: Pen and paper.

DESCRIPTION: A student writes down where he was at a certain time in the past and challenges the class to guess where he was.

For example:

"Where was I at noon yesterday?"
"Were you at the dentist?"
"No, I wasn't at the dentist."

ADAPTATION: To review other persons, the challenger could ask:

"Where was Gary last Tuesday?"

or

"Where were Joan and I last Sunday?"

or

"Where were you and I last night?"

SUGGESTION: I limit the number of questions to one-half the number of students in the group (or 20). If the location has not been guessed by that time, it is revealed, and the challenger is replaced by another.

19. GUESSER

L, S, R, W

level: beginners
optimal group size: 20

OBJECTIVE: To give students practice describing people.

MATERIALS NEEDED: Blackboard and chalk.

DESCRIPTION: The GUESSER has his back to the blackboard as the teacher writes the name of another student on it for the class to see, and then quickly erases the name. The GUESSER chooses some students to describe the person whose name was written. The clues start by being general and then narrowing down to the specific. When the person's identity is guessed, a new round is begun.

SUGGESTIONS: In order to ensure that the clues go from the general to the specific, I have my students tell about the mystery person's sex, hair colour, height, eye colour, weight, and other general characteristics first. It helps if those features are written on the board for the students to follow.

To make the game even more challenging, we frequently blindfold the GUESSER.

I usually set a limit on the number of clues given for each round (10, in most cases).

20. YES/NO PING-PONG

L, S

level: beginners
optimal group size: unlimited

OBJECTIVE: To give students practice asking and answering questions that require YES/NO answers.

MATERIALS NEEDED: None.

DESCRIPTION: The class is divided into 2 teams (A and B). Students, in turn, ask their opponents questions to which only YES or NO is the answer.

A point is won for each correct question and for every appropriate answer. Once a student answers a question, he poses one to his questioner. For example:

A1: Do you speak English?
B1: Yes, I do.

B1: Can you ride a bike?
A1: Yes, I can.

A2: Is your sister here?
B2: No, she isn't.

B2: Do you know my name?
A2: Yes, I do.

21. PREPOSITIONS

L, S

level: beginners
optimal group size: unlimited

OBJECTIVE: To assess and strengthen students' knowledge and use of prepositions.

MATERIALS NEEDED: Paper and pencil.

DESCRIPTION: The teacher instructs the class to draw various geometric shapes in certain places on their pages and to place numbers and letters **IN, ON, UNDER, TO** THE LEFT **OF, IN** THE BOTTOM RIGHT HAND CORNER **OF,** etc, the shapes. Results are compared with the teacher's copy, and the person with the fewest errors takes his turn at instructing the class.

Examples:

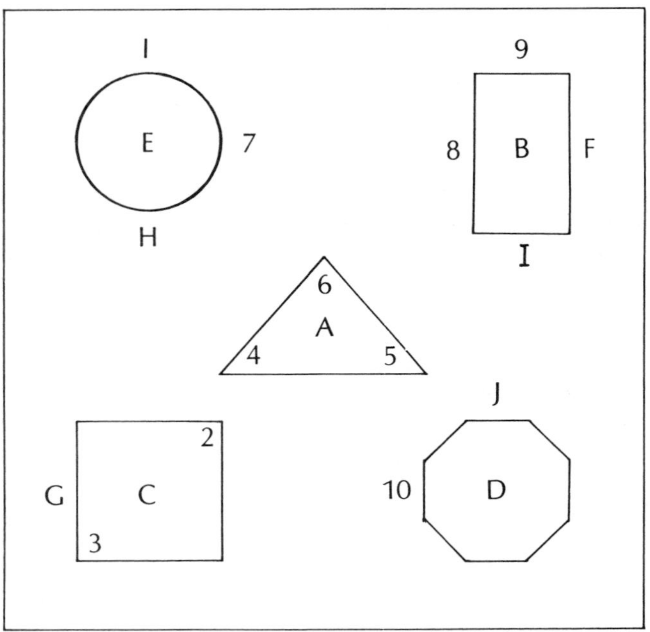

22. TIC-TAC-WEATHER

L, S

level: beginners
optimal group size: 20

OBJECTIVE: To review weather conditions.

MATERIALS NEEDED: The following grid on the overhead.

DESCRIPTION: The group is divided into 2 teams (Team X and Team O). The first player of Team X chooses a position, identifies it by number, and describes the weather condition in that space. If he is correct, his team marker is placed there and his team occupies that position. If an error is made, the position remains vacant until it is correctly identified. The first team to occupy 3 positions in a row (vertically, horizontally, or diagonally) wins.

The central position can be gained, at any time, by stating the negative form of any other position; for example, "It isn't raining."

23. HERE AND THERE

L, S

level: beginners
optimal group size: 20

OBJECTIVE: To reinforce the meaning and use of HERE and THERE.

MATERIALS NEEDED: Each student supplies several (2 to 5) objects, such as a notebook, ruler, comb, shoe, etc.

DESCRIPTION: The objects are divided into 2 piles which are placed at opposite ends of the room. One-half of the group searches one pile for their belongings, while the other half explores the other pile for theirs. (Articles not found in one pile are assumed to be in the other pile).

Students take turns indicating the location of their possessions by pointing and saying, for example:

> "My pen is HERE." (He indicates the pile he is looking through.) "My shoe is THERE." (He points to the pile at the far end of the room.)

24. FISH!

L, S, (R)

level: beginners
optimal group size: unlimited

OBJECTIVE: To review the verb TO HAVE in the Present Indicative, using the interrogative, affirmative, and negative forms. In addition, the names of the playing cards are learned.

MATERIALS NEEDED: One deck of playing cards for every 4 or 5 students in the class. (Cards can be provided by students.)

DESCRIPTION: Students are grouped in 4s or 5s and each one is dealt 5 cards. The remaining cards are turned face-down in a pile in the centre of the group. The first person to the left of the dealer asks anyone in the group for cards **already in his hand** – the object being to get four of a kind (that is, 4 Queens, or four 3s, etc). A player continues to ask as long as he receives the card(s) asked for, whether from another student, or when told to fish from the inverted pile. The turn to ask continues around the group to the left until somebody gets 4 of a kind. Then the cards are re-shuffled and re-dealt for a new round. For example:

Student A: "Do you have any ______s?"
Student B: "No, I don't have any ______s. Fish!"

(Whereupon, Student A takes the top card from the inverted pile in the centre of the group. If it is the card he had asked for, he continues to ask for any card already in his hand. If not, the turn goes to the player on his left.)

Student C: "Do you have any ______s?"
Student D: "Yes I do."

Student C: "How many ______s do you have?"
Student D: "I have 1/2/3 ______(s)."

Student C: "May I have it/them, please?"
Student D: "Here you are." (Hands C the card/s.)

Student C: "Thank you."
Student D: "You're welcome."

(Student C, having received the card(s) asked for, continues to ask for more cards.)

SUGGESTIONS: When I teach the dialogue to my students, I have the entire class repeat after me (showing them the card being asked for so they learn the cards as they learn the dialogue). After several repetitions, using various cards, I have one-half the class ask the other half, then they exchange roles. This is repeated several times.

With some classes, I give them the dialogue on paper and, together, we read it several times. I tell them to use the sheets during the game, and when they feel confident they can turn them face-down on their desks. I then walk among them as they play, monitor their facility with the dialogue, and collect papers which have been placed face-down.

Students of all backgrounds have difficulty distinguishing between "ace" and "eight," singular and plural. I make sure to give them lots of practice during the drill.

To make the game a bit more exciting, I give each student 5 paper clips. At the beginning of each round, each player "antes up" (puts one clip in a pile in the centre of the group) and the winner collects all of them.

25. PROFESSIONS

L, S

level: beginners
optimal group size: 10

OBJECTIVE: To review various professions.
MATERIALS NEEDED: None.
DESCRIPTION: One student leaves the room while the rest of the group decides on a PROFESSION. When he returns, the other students say one sentence which describes the PROFESSION, while he tries to guess it. Examples:

Student 1: "He works with many people."
Student 2: "He talks a lot."
Student 3: "He writes a lot."
Student 4: "He gets angry a lot."

Student 5: "He laughs a lot."
Student 6: "He uses a lot of chalk."

(The answer is 'teacher'.)

Student 1: "He fixes things."
Student 2: "He charges a lot."
Student 3: "You call him for emergencies."
Student 4: "He comes to your house."
Student 5: "He works with water."
Student 6: "He uses wrenches."
Student 7: "He fixes sinks and toilets."

(The answer is 'plumber'.)

26. WHO HAS IT?

L, S

level: beginners
optimal group size: unlimited

OBJECTIVE: To reinforce the use of the verb TO HAVE in the Simple Present tense (interrogative, affirmative, and negative).

MATERIALS NEEDED: A small object (such as a button, coin, or paper clip).

DESCRIPTION: The class is divided into 2 teams (A and B). Team A leaves the room while the small object is given to one member of Team B. When Team A returns, members of Team A take turns asking members of Team B – WHO HAS IT? For example:

A1: "Do you have it, Paul?"
Paul: "No, I don't have it."

A2: "Does Marie have it, Robert?"
Robert: "No, Marie doesn't have it."

A3: "Does Carl have it, Linda?"
Linda: "No, Carl doesn't have it."

A4: "Do you have it, Sharon?"
Sharon: "Yes, I have it."

The number of questions posed is limited to one-half the number of players on each team.

A point is awarded to Team A if the possessor is guessed, whereas Team B wins a point if the possessor is not guessed within the limited number of questions. The teams change roles when the possessor is guessed, or when all questions are used up.

27. FAMILY

W, L, S

level: beginners
optimal group size: unlimited

OBJECTIVE: To review familial relationships.

MATERIALS NEEDED: Pen and paper for each student.

DESCRIPTION: Students pair off and challenge their opponents to state the familial relationship. For example:

Student 1: John is Louise's uncle. Who is Louise?
Student 2: Louise is John's niece.

Student 2: Carol is Susan's mother. Who is Susan?
Student 1: Susan is Carol's daughter.

Scoring: One point for each correct response.

SUGGESTION: I have found that this works more smoothly if the challenges are written down before they are presented. This avoids confusion and lapses of memory.

28. TIC-TAC-BEFORE-AND-AFTER

L, S, R

level: beginners
optimal group size: 20

OBJECTIVE: To review and reinforce the concepts of BEFORE and AFTER.

MATERIALS NEEDED: The following grid on the overhead or the blackboard.

a/b	6/7	4/5
2/3	d/e	c/d
p/q	8/9	9/10

DESCRIPTION: The group is divided into 2 teams (Team X and Team O). The first player chooses a position on the grid and tells the relation of one letter or number to the other. For example:

A is *before* B.
Seven is *after* six.

If he is correct, his team symbol (X or O) is placed in that position. If he is incorrect, the position remains vacant until it is correctly identified. To win, a team has to place three of its symbols in a row – vertically, horizontally, or diagonally.

29. ODD AND EVEN RESULTS

L, S, R, W

level: beginners
optimal group size: unlimited

OBJECTIVE: To review cardinal numbers.

MATERIALS NEEDED: Pencil and paper for each student.

DESCRIPTION: Students are paired off; one of them takes ODD and the other takes EVEN. They both write down any number (within a prescribed range, if you prefer) without seeing each other's number. The 2 numbers are added together and if the result is EVEN, the player who chose EVEN wins a point; if the result is ODD, the player who chose ODD receives the point. The first person to earn 10 points wins.

For example, the range is 20 to 50:

Player A (ODD)		Player B (EVEN)			
26	+	45	=	71	(ODD player wins 1 point.)
43	+	50	=	93	(ODD player wins 1 point.)
36	+	22	=	58	(EVEN player wins 1 point.)
21	+	43	=	64	(EVEN player wins 1 point.)

ADAPTATION: Subtraction could be used to provide a little variety.

30. RHYME PING-PONG

L, S

level: beginners
optimal group size: unlimited

OBJECTIVE: To expand vocabulary.

MATERIALS NEEDED: None.

DESCRIPTION: Students pair off and the first of each pair says a word to his opponent who must respond with a rhyming word. They volley back and forth until one cannot think of an ORIGINAL rhyming word. His opponent then wins a point, and the loser begins the next round with a new word. For example:

Student 1:	man		pan		ran		YOU WIN!
Student 2:		tan		fan		can	

Student 1:	sick		lick		quick		
Student 2:		thick		trick		YOU WIN!	

Student 2:	wood		good		YOU WIN!
Student 1:		should		could	

SUGGESTION: Have the students spell each word after saying it. This expands the opponent's vocabulary and ensures that there is no confusion with homonyms (for example, "wood" and "would"). Furthermore, it is a good exercise in spelling for all.

31. BODY STRETCHER

L

level: beginners
optimal group size: unlimited

OBJECTIVE: To review parts of the body.

MATERIALS NEEDED: None.

DESCRIPTION: Students are paired off. One names 3 parts of the body. When he has finished, the other must touch them in the order named. Then the roles are reversed. One point for each correct response. For example:

"Touch your nose, knee and elbow."

When both participants have done 3 parts, 4 are named and touched; then 5, and 6 . . .

Only parts which are touched in the order called are worth a point each.

SUGGESTION: Students could write the body parts before the game is played in order to avoid confusion and arguments. For example:

(1) nose (2) knee (3) elbow
(1) ear (2) toes (3) shoulder (4) wrist
(1) chin (2) back (3) thumb (4) ankle (5) eye
(1) finger (2) arm (3) leg (4) shoulder (5) foot (6) mouth

32. WORD CALLING

R, S

level: beginners
optimal group size: unlimited

OBJECTIVE: To increase speed of word recognition.

MATERIALS NEEDED: Flashcards of familiar words; as many cards as there are students. One word per card.

DESCRIPTION: The class is divided into 2 teams (A and B). A flashcard is shown very quickly and briefly to one member of each team simultaneously. The first person to call out the word wins a point for his team. This continues down the ranks until each has had 2 turns.

SUGGESTIONS: This works more smoothly if each competitor is equidistant from the teacher as the flashcard is briskly displayed. The easiest method is to have each team line up on opposite sides of the room, curving into the centre and up towards the teacher.

Example:

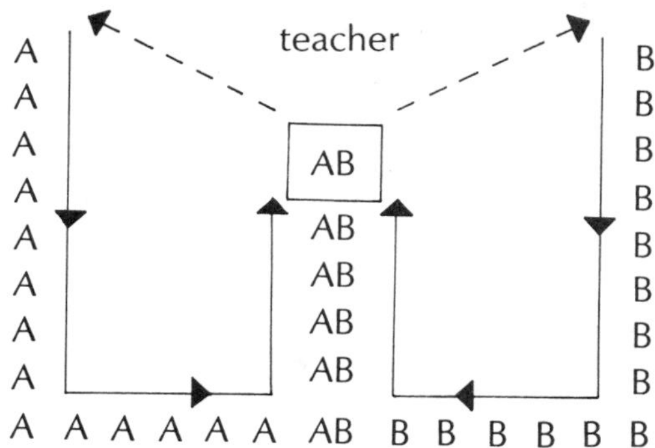

The teacher is the judge whose decision is final. Questioning the judge's decision will cost your team 5 points.

33. I SPY

L, S

level: beginners
optimal group size: 20

OBJECTIVE: To review vocabulary (and spelling).

MATERIALS NEEDED: None.

DESCRIPTION: One student challenges the group to guess what he sees in the room.

"I spy (with my little eye) something that is green. What is it?"

"Is it the chalkboard?"
"No, it isn't the chalkboard."

"Is it the wastebasket?"
"No, it isn't the wastebasket."

Once one-half the number of students in the group have guessed, the object is revealed and a new challenger is chosen.

ADAPTATION: If spelling practice is needed, students could spell the names of objects instead of saying them. For example:

"I spy something that begins with a 'B'. What is it?"

"Is it a B-O-O-K?"
"No, it isn't a B-O-O-K."

"Is it a B-O-Y?"
"No, it isn't a B-O-Y."

"Is it a B-A-G?"
"Yes, it is a B-A-G."

34. PREPOSITIONAL PICTURES

L, S

level: beginners
optimal group size: unlimited

OBJECTIVE: To reinforce the use of prepositions of place.

MATERIALS NEEDED: Paper and pencil for each student.

DESCRIPTION: The teacher describes a scene to the class who draw what is being described. For example:

> "In the centre of the page, there is a house. There is a chimney on the left side of the roof, and a window on the right side of the house. In the upper right hand corner of the page, there is a cloud. There is a tall tree to the left of the house, and a sidewalk in front. A small dog is standing on the grass, to the right of the sidewalk. He has a big bone in his mouth . . ."

SUGGESTION: After I have dictated 10 to 15 details, I divide the class into groups of 5 to 7 players, and each player takes a turn dictating 2 additional details which the others in his group draw. Then, each in turn asks 2 questions about the picture. For example:

> "Where is the dog? What is in the tree?"

This gives each student a chance to speak during the game.

35. WHERE IS IT?

L, S

level: beginners
optimal group size: unlimited

OBJECTIVE: To reinforce the use of IT IS in the interrogative, negative, and affirmative; and to reinforce the use of prepositions.

MATERIALS NEEDED: A small object, such as a coin, a button or a paper clip.

DESCRIPTION: A student leaves the room while the class hides the small object. When he returns, he tries to find where it is hidden by asking a few students questions like:

"Is it under the desk, Rob?"
"No, it isn't under the desk."

"Is it in your shoe, Jackie?"
"No, it isn't in my shoe."

"Is it behind the door, Gary?"
"Yes, it is behind the door."

If the object has not been found by the time a limited number of questions have been posed, the guesser is told its location and a new guesser is chosen for a new round.

SUGGESTION: I usually limit the number of questions to one-half the number of students in the class, or 20 maximum.

36. TIC-TAC-MATH

L, S

level: beginners
optimal group size: 20

OBJECTIVE: To review and reinforce the use of cardinal numbers with the aid of arithmetic operations.

MATERIALS NEEDED: The following grid on the overhead projector or the blackboard.

A. 6 + 8 =	B. 9 × 2 =	C. 14 − 9 =
D. 18 ÷ 6 =	E. 12 − 9 =	F. 10 + 6 =
G. 19 + 9 =	H. 20 ÷ 4 =	I. 6 × 7 =

DESCRIPTION: The group is divided into 2 teams (Team X and Team O). The first player chooses a position on the grid and describes the arithmetic operation occupying that position. For example:

"Space A: Six plus eight equals fourteen."

If correct, his team symbol (X or O) is placed in that space. If wrong, the position remains vacant until someone correctly describes the arithmetic operation there. The first team to gain 3 positions in a row (vertically, horizontally, or diagonally) wins.

ADAPTATION: Sometimes, when we play this game, students are required to spell the number words in each operation described.

37. WHAT HAPPENED?

L, S

level: beginners
optimal group size: unlimited

OBJECTIVE: To review the Simple Past in the interrogative, affirmative, and negative.

MATERIALS NEEDED: Cards with a simple sentence in the past tense on each. Examples:

Last night I had a terrible accident.
Yesterday, I screamed at my children.
My brother sold his new car last week.
We went to a Japanese restaurant for dinner.

DESCRIPTION: A student takes a card and reads the sentence to the class. The others take turns asking him questions to which he fabricates answers. For example:

Where were you?
Who was with you?
What time did it happen?
What did you do?
Why did you do that?
How did you do it?

SUGGESTION: I usually limit the number of questions to one-half the number of students in the group (or 20). When the limit has been reached, a new student reads a new card to the group.

38. ODD OR EVEN?

L, S, (R, W)

level: beginners
optimal group size: unlimited

OBJECTIVE: To review cardinal numbers.

MATERIALS NEEDED: At least 20 small objects (such as paper clips or hole reinforcements) for each student.

DESCRIPTION: Students are paired off. One holds a handful of objects and asks his opponent, "ODD OR EVEN?" His opponent makes a choice and, together, they count the objects. If the result is odd, the player who chose ODD wins a point. If the result is even, the player who chose EVEN wins a point. The other player holds the objects for the next round.

SUGGESTION: To provide practice in spelling out the numbers, students could keep score as follows:

Number	Odd/Even	Point
nine	odd	Mike
fifteen	odd	Susan
twelve	even	Susan
nineteen	odd	Mike
sixteen	even	Susan

The first player to reach 10 points wins.

39. SOUND OFF

L, R

level: beginners
optimal group size: unlimited

OBJECTIVE: To develop auditory discrimination.

MATERIALS NEEDED: Each student has 2 sound cards (each containing a word with one of the two sounds being contrasted).

For the example, we'll use / ɛ / and / a /. Example: BET BAT

DESCRIPTION: The class is divided into 2 teams. The teacher reads words containing one or the other sound and students are to hold up the matching sound card. Example:

Teacher: "met"............................... Students hold up BET

Teacher: "mat"............................... Students hold up BAT

Teacher: "fat"................................ Students hold up BAT

Teacher: "set"................................ Students hold up BET

Teacher: "less"................................ Students hold up BET

Teacher: "last"................................ Students hold up BAT

The team with more correct responses each round earns 1 point.

SUGGESTIONS: I have my students make their sound cards, but I advise them to use one colour for one sound and another colour for the other (red for BET and blue for BAT, for example). The colour contrast facilitates counting similar responses. Any two sounds, which students have difficulty distinguishing between, can be contrasted. Here are a few of the ones that I have used: B**E**T/B**I**T; **TH**OSE/**D**OZE: **TH**REE/**T**REE: C**U**T/C**O**T and **L**EAD/**R**EAD.

40. DESCRIPTION

L, S

level: beginners
optimal group size: 20

OBJECTIVE: To give students practice in describing people.

MATERIALS NEEDED: None.

DESCRIPTION: The group is divided into 2 teams (A and B). Team A describes one member of the opposing team without revealing the person's name. Each member of Team A gives 1 detail about the person being described, while members of Team B take turns trying to guess his identity after each detail is given.

The scoring can be done in one of two ways:

(1) The describing team gains 1 point for each detail that they must give before the guessing team identifies the mystery person.

OR

(2) The guessing team starts out with 10 points and loses 1 for each detail it needs before it can guess the identity of the mystery person. Once they have been reduced to zero, the identity is revealed, and the roles are reversed.

41. DARTS

L, S

level: beginners
optimal group size: unlimited

OBJECTIVE: To review cardinal numbers.

MATERIALS NEEDED: One dartsheet (with 5 dartboards on each side), and one pencil for each student.

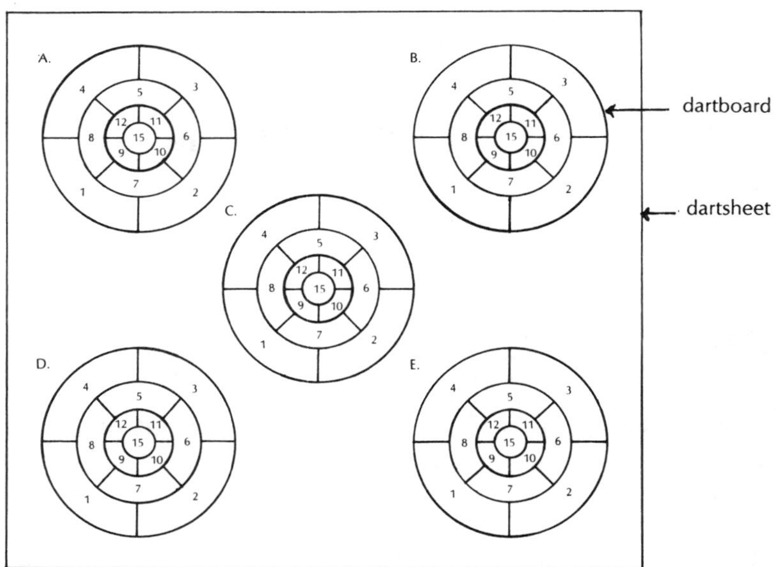

DESCRIPTION: Students pair off and one takes his turn touching a dartboard with his pencil (eyes closed) 10 times. His score is totalled aloud. Then his opponent takes his turn. The higher score wins each match.

SUGGESTION: I draw 5 dartboards on each side of each sheet of paper to make the best use of the paper, and to give students lots of practice.

42. SIT FOR SOUNDS

L

level: beginners
optimal group size: unlimited

OBJECTIVE: To improve auditory discrimination.

MATERIALS NEEDED: Appropriate word lists as described below.

DESCRIPTION: All students are told to stand. The teacher says:

> "I'm going to say 4 words. Sit down when you hear one that begins with the sound /ð/ as in **TH**IS. Ready? DISH. VERY. THAT. THICK."

Only students who sat down correctly are allowed to remain seated for the next round, **OR** all students are told to stand for each new round. The method you choose will depend on whether you want to concentrate on students who have difficulty discriminating between particular sounds (others remain seated), or give everybody equal practice in auditory discrimination. Sounds in initial, medial and terminal positions can be used at different times.

A good practice is to contrast voiced and unvoiced sounds: **v/f**; **g/k**;**d/t**;**b/p**; **z/s**;**ǰ/č**;**ž/š**;**ð/θ**; and the **l/r** contrast.

SUGGESTION: Once students become proficient, I perform the same exercise with my back to the group. This eliminates the visual clue as to how the sound is produced. This gives us the opportunity to contrast sounds like **s/f/θ** and **z/v/ð**.

43. NINETY-EIGHT

L, S

level: beginners
optimal group size: unlimited

OBJECTIVE: To review cardinal numbers.

MATERIALS NEEDED: Three paper clips per student and several decks of playing cards (1 deck for every 4 or 5 students). The cards can be supplied by the students.

DESCRIPTION: Players take turns discarding cards and adding their values up to a **maximum of 98.** When the value of the discarded cards reaches 98, the next player must have a special card (**King, 10, 9** or **5**) to continue. The player without a special card can't play his hand and loses that round, paying 1 of his 3 paper clips to the "kitty."

All cards have their face value, except the following four **SPECIAL CARDS: KING** = automatic 98; **10** = minus 10; **9** = no change; and **5** = reverse direction. (The Ace is worth 1 and the Queen and Jack are worth 10 each.)

Students are grouped in 4s or 5s and each one is dealt 5 cards. The rest of the cards are placed face-down in a pile, around which the players sit. The player to the left of the dealer (A, in the following example) discards a card (usually his biggest regular card – Q, J, 8, 7, etc) and calls out the value of that card. He then picks one up from the inverted pile in the centre (so that he always has 5 cards in his hand). Each player to his left (B, C, and D in the example) discards a card in turn and adds its value to the accumulated value of the previously discarded cards.

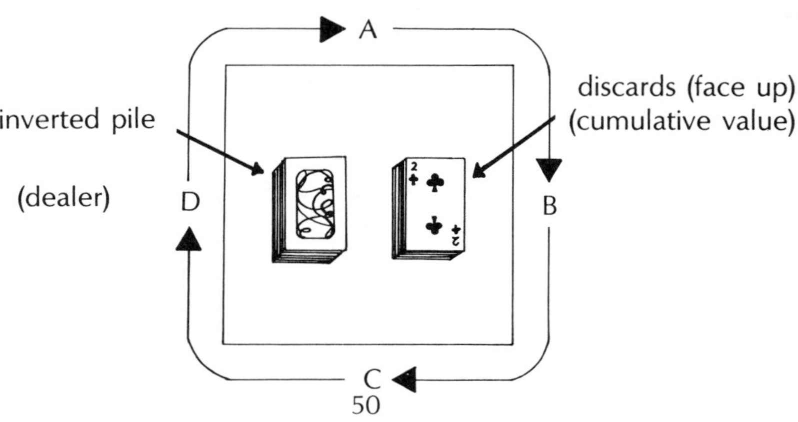

Play continues until the value of the discard pile reaches 98. Ninety-eight is the MAXIMUM PERMISSIBLE VALUE of the pile of discards. Now is when the special cards are needed. If it is your turn, and the value is 98, and you don't have any special cards (**K, 10, 9** or **5**), you are stuck and lose the round since any other card will raise the value over 98.

Suppose, for example, player C discards a card that brings the value of the pile to 96. It is now player D's turn. He has to discard a card which will not raise the value of the pile over 98. He could use a special card (**King** = automatic 98, **10** = minus 10, **9** = no change, or **5** = reverse direction), or he could use an Ace (=1) or a 2 (=2), but nothing more than a 2 since anything more would raise the value over 98. Suppose he has a 2 and plays it. That brings the value up to 98, and it is now A's turn. Player A must now have a special card to survive, since *any other card* would raise the value over 98. Suppose he plays a **9** (no change). The value remains 98 and the turn advances to player B. If B plays a **5** (reverse direction), this would reverse the turn back to A (value still 98), and the turn would continue in that direction (to the right) until someone reverses it again (using a **5**). If A deposits a **10** (= minus 10), that would reduce the value by 10 to 88 for D.

D could now play **any** card since nothing would raise the value more than 10 points to over 98. D could now dump his biggest card (suppose it was a 7), and raise the value to 95 (88 + 7 = 95) for C. Suppose C had the following cards in his hand: 4, 6, 6, 8, Q. He would be stuck, since even his smallest card, the 4, would raise the value over 98. He would, therefore, lose that round, and would pay 1 of the 3 paper clips that he started with. The cards are shuffled and re-dealt, this time by A, and B would begin the next round by discarding his biggest card.

When a player has lost all 3 of his paper clips, he is out. The last player with any paper clips (that is, all the others have lost all 3) is the winner.

SUGGESTIONS: I advise my students to arrange their hands so that special cards (**K, 10, 9, 5**) and low value cards (A, 2, 3) are reserved on the left for emergencies, while big regular cards (Q, J, 8, 7, 6) are on the right.

For example:

I project the values of the special cards on the overhead so that students have a constant reminder of which cards are special, and their respective values. Special cards can be used at anytime, but are of most value in emergencies (when the value is close to 98).

Suppose I am dealt the following cards: **K, 9, 9, 10, 6**. Four of those 5 cards are special. When it my turn to discard, I would probably lay down a **King** and automatically raise the value of the pile to 98, no matter what its value was. I would feel pretty secure in doing so, since the odds are that the next player won't have a special card, and will lose immediately. Even if he had a **5** and reversed the direction back to me, I would have several options open to me: **9** would pass the 98 on to the next player, and **10** would lower the value to 88. In any case, *I* would be off the hook, and someone else would lose.

Each time I introduce the game to students, I "play" with 3 other players, open-handed (cards visible to all), while the rest of the class look on. I think <u>out loud</u> for each player in turn and play for each one in turn. Then the class breaks up into groups of 4 or 5 students and each group plays amongst themselves.

44. FLASHWORDS

R, W

levels: beginners & intermediate
optimal group size: unlimited

OBJECTIVE: To assess and improve word-recognition ability.

MATERIALS NEEDED: An overhead projector and many (50 or more) familiar words on strips of acetate.

DESCRIPTION: Several words (5 to 20) are shown briefly to the class and then are concealed. The student who can recall and write down the greatest number of words correctly chooses the new words for the next round.

SUGGESTIONS: Having the words on strips of transparent acetate makes it easy to control the number of words on the projector. Turning off the projector, after showing the words, conceals them.

Also, I find it works best to begin with 5 words and make the game progressively more challenging by increasing the number of words by 1 for each successive round.

45. RHYME MIME

L, S

level: beginners & intermediate
optimal group size: 20

OBJECTIVE: To review and reinforce vocabulary.

MATERIALS NEEDED: None.

DESCRIPTION: The group is divided into 2 teams. One player thinks of 2 rhyming words and acts them out for his team. A time limit is imposed (1 to 2 minutes, depending on your students' abilities), and 1 point is won for each word guessed within the time limit. When Team A is finished, Team B takes its turn.

For example:

SHIP + TRIP
HOT + POT
SEW + THROW
SIGN + SHINE
SNOB + SLOB

SUGGESTION: If one team cannot guess one or both words before the time expires, the other team can make 1 guess earning 1 point for each correct word. This encourages the inactive team to pay attention to the other team's activities.

46. RAILROAD SPELLING

L, S

levels: beginners & intermediate
optimal group size: unlimited

OBJECTIVE: To reinforce spelling skills.

MATERIALS NEEDED: None.

DESCRIPTION: The group is divided into 2 teams (A and B). The first person of Team A says and spells a word (any word), and the first person on Team B must say and spell a word that begins with the last letter of the preceding word. One point for each word correctly spelled. Repetitions are not permitted. The teams alternate turns down the ranks. For example:

A1: hello, h-e-l-l-**o**
B1: **o**range, o-r-a-n-g-**e**
A2: **e**asy, e-a-s-**y**
B2: **y**es, y-e-**s**
A3: **s**top, s-t-o-**p**
B3: **p**lease, p-l-e-a-s-**e**

SUGGESTION: I usually restrict acceptable words by limiting the minimum number of letters. For example, all words must be at least 5 letters long.

47. SLIDES AND LADDERS

L, S

levels: beginners & intermediate
optimal group size: 10
(For larger groups, see SUGGESTION.)

OBJECTIVE: To review and reinforce the use of cardinal numbers and/or to review grammar and test general knowledge.

MATERIALS NEEDED: A SLIDES AND LADDERS board (made by the teacher or by students) and a number spinner (or a deck of playing cards, or a pair of dice). If you use cards, the ace is worth 1 point and the picture cards are worth 10 points each.

←	100	99	98	97	96	95	94	93	92	91
	81	82	83	84	85	86	87	88	89	90
	80	79	78	77	76	75	74	73	72	71
	61	62	63	64	65	66	67	68	69	70
	60	59	58	57	56	55	54	53	52	51
	41	42	43	44	45	46	47	48	49	50
	40	39	38	37	36	35	34	33	32	31
	21	22	23	24	25	26	27	28	29	30
	20	19	18	17	16	15	14	13	12	11
→	1	2	3	4	5	6	7	8	9	10

11 12 1
10 2
9 3
8 4
7 6 5

Number Spinner

DESCRIPTION: Students take turns placing a marker on the starting space and spinning the number spinner (or drawing a card, or tossing the dice). They then move their marker the appropriate number of spaces. Depending on their ability, they could (1) call out the spun (drawn or tossed) number and/or (2) say their destination and/or (3) orally add the spun number to their present position (5 + 7 = 12, for example). If you land at the base of a ladder as in the example (5 + 7 = 12), you climb up to the top of the ladder (in this case, 50) and continue from there on your next turn. If, however, you land at the top of a slide (28, for instance), you slide down to the bottom of the slide (7) and continue from there on your next turn. The first person past 100, or the person leading when time expires, wins.

ADAPTATION: For students who don't need practice with their numbers, I have them answer a question (on grammar or general knowledge) before they are permitted to spin and move.

SUGGESTION: I have 4 SLIDES AND LADDERS boards and divide my class into 4 groups, so that 4 games can be played simultaneously. This eliminates long, tedious lulls while each student waits for his next turn.

Note: In various parts of the country, this game is also known as Snakes and Ladders or Chutes and Ladders. I feel that SLIDES AND LADDERS is a more meaningful name.

48. NAME THE NOUNS

L, S, R, W

levels: beginners & intermediate
optimal group size: unlimited

OBJECTIVE: To give students practice in identifying nouns in context.

MATERIALS NEEDED: Each student writes 10 sentences of varying length.

DESCRIPTION: Students are paired off. They take turns reading one of their original sentences to their opponent and challenging him to name all the nouns in the sentence. The opponent gains 1 point for each noun correctly identified. Then the opponent reads one of his sentences and challenges the other to name all the nouns in his sentence.

SUGGESTION: If your students are able, you could have them state the type of noun each one is. For example, common (dog), proper (France), abstract (fear), and collective (crowd).

49. ALPHABET DASH

S

levels: beginners & intermediate
optimal group size: 20

OBJECTIVE: To review vocabulary.

MATERIALS NEEDED: Cards numbered 1 to 20.

DESCRIPTION: The group is divided into 2 teams of 10 players each. Each player is given a numbered card. The teacher calls out a number and a letter and the student with that number has 20 seconds to name as many words as possible that start with that letter. His team gets one point for each correct word.

SUGGESTION: From time to time we play this game with a restriction on the words called out. For example, they can be restricted to verbs, names of countries, or must have at least 2 syllables.

50. SPELLING BASEBALL

L, S

levels: beginners & intermediate
optimal group size: unlimited

OBJECTIVE: To reinforce spelling ability.

MATERIALS NEEDED: An appropriate spelling list.

DESCRIPTION: Three bases and home plate are indicated in the room (masking tape on the floor or specially designated desks). The class is divided into 2 equal teams. One team (Team A) sits in the "dugout" (on one side of the room) while one member of the team is at bat. The pitchers (students on Team B) sit in the centre of the "diamond" and call out words from the list that the batters, in turn, must spell.

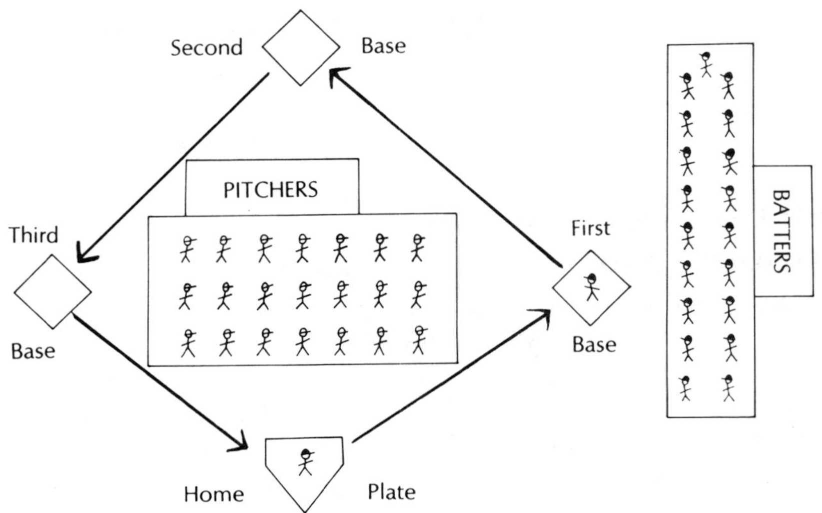

To start the game, a coin is tossed to determine which team will pitch and which will be at bat first. Batter #1 stands at HOME PLATE while pitcher #1 gives him a word to spell. If he spells it correctly, he moves to FIRST BASE. If wrong, he is out. The next batter comes to HOME PLATE and is given a word by the next pitcher. If he is correct, he moves to FIRST BASE and any batters at bases move ahead 1 base. A point is counted each time a batter comes HOME. When 3 batters are out, the teams change places.

SUGGESTION: I stipulate that if one team is inattentive, or disrupts the game in any way, the other team is automatically given a point.

51. HANDS UP!

L, S

levels: beginners & intermediate
optimal group size: 10

OBJECTIVE: To develop critical listening skills, and reinforce understanding of question words.

MATERIALS NEEDED: None.

DESCRIPTION: The teacher reads (or makes up) sentences to the group. At the end of each sentence, students raise their hands to offer to identify as many question words and answers as possible. One point for each question word and 1 for each answer. For example:

Teacher	–"Henry speaks clearly."	
Student 1	–"WHO? Henry."	(2 points)
	"HOW? Clearly."	(2 points)
		(TOTAL: 4 points)
Teacher	–"The dog barked loudly in the back yard all night."	
Student 2	–"WHO? The dog."	(2 points)
	"WHERE? In the back yard."	(2 points)
	"HOW? Loudly."	(2 points)
		(TOTAL: 6 points)

Any errors or omissions are worth double to other students:

Student 3	–"He forgot WHEN. All night."	(4 points)

52. STOP!

R, W

levels: beginners & intermediate
optimal group size: unlimited

OBJECTIVE: To enhance students' abilities in spelling and word recognition.

MATERIALS NEEDED: Paper and pencil.

DESCRIPTION: Students are paired off and one thinks of a word (any word). He puts dashes on the paper representing the letters of the word. His opponent tries to guess the letters of the word and, eventually, the word itself. For example:

"Is there an E in your word?"

If "yes", all Es are written in their respective positions.

If "no", one-half of the S of STOP! is formed as a penalty.

In either case, the E is crossed out in the alphabet at the bottom of the page to show that it has already been guessed. The guesser can make 10 mistakes before STOP! is formed and the game ends.

If the word is discovered before STOP! is formed, the guesser wins. If STOP! is formed before the word is guessed, the challenger wins. Students alternate roles with every new match.

Example:

_ O S _ I _ A L

~~A~~ ~~B~~ C D ~~E~~ F ~~G~~ H ~~I~~ J K ~~L~~ M

N ~~O~~ P Q ~~R~~ ~~S~~ T ~~U~~ V W X Y Z

In the above example, at this point in the challenge, the opponent has made 10 guesses, shown by the 10 letters crossed out at the bottom. Five guesses have been correct (the O, S, I, A and L written into their places in the word), and 5 wrong (indicated by the five half-letters in the incomplete STOP!)

Note: If you are familiar with the game Hangman, yes, STOP! is quite similar. I have modified Hangman to limit to 10 the number of wrong guesses each player can make. With Hangman, I have seen some players hanged after only 5 wrong guesses, while others survive 15 to 20, depending on the complexity of the drawing of the hanged man. With STOP!, each player has the same chance. Besides, capital punishment is no longer in vogue in this country.

53. TWENTY QUESTIONS

L, S

levels: beginners & intermediate
optimal group size: unlimited

OBJECTIVE: To strengthen the ability to ask and answer questions that require YES/NO answers.

MATERIALS NEEDED: None.

DESCRIPTION: One student thinks of a concrete noun (BOAT, for example). The others can ask him up to 20 questions that require YES/NO answers in an attempt to discover the identity of his noun. The person who correctly guesses the noun replaces the challenger. If the noun is not guessed by the time 20 questions have been posed, it is revealed, and a new round is begun by a new challenger chosen by the teacher.

ADAPTATION: I divide classes of more than 30 students into 4 equal teams. One team decides on a noun and members of the other 3 teams try to guess its identity. The group which guesses correctly wins a point, and the next team, in turn, challenges the others. This team effort enables greater individual involvement and increases each student's interest in the game.

SUGGESTION: I have the challenger write his noun on a piece of paper to avoid problems (such as forgetting or changing his word).

Note: Questions must elicit only YES/NO answers.

For example, the question can be: "Is it bigger than this desk?" It cannot be general in nature, such as, "How big is it?" Nor are OR questions permitted, for example, "Is it big or small?" I make this clear to my students by stating that the only acceptable answers are "Yes" and "No." The challenger can't give any more information than a simple "Yes" or "No." MAYBE questions (that is, questions to which "Yes" and "No" are equally correct responses) could be disregarded when counting the 20 questions. This allows for more direct questioning and gives questioners a better chance of discovering the identity of the noun.

4. HEADS AND TAILS

L, S, (R, W)

levels: beginners & intermediate
optimal group size: unlimited

OBJECTIVE: To expand vocabulary.

MATERIALS NEEDED: None, but blackboard or overhead is optional.

DESCRIPTION: The class is divided into any number of equal teams. The first player calls out a word, **any word**, and the first player on the next team must call out a word which begins with the last letter of the previous word. This continues from team to team until someone cannot think of an original, suitable word. He, then, loses a point for his team, and the player of the next team gains 2 points for his team if he comes up with an acceptable word.

Example: ELEPHAN[T]
[T]RE[E]
[E]A[T]
[T]ONGU[E]
[E]AC[H]
[H]APP[Y]
[Y]ES . . .

ADAPTATION: To make the game more challenging, especially with Intermediate classes, I often restrict the words used to specific categories such as countries, verbs, or singers.

SUGGESTION: I try to enforce the rule that each word can be used **only once.** This is facilitated if the words are written, as they are called out, on the blackboard or overhead projector by the teacher or a student.

55. THREE WORDS

L, S, R, W

levels: beginners & intermediate
optimal group size: unlimited

OBJECTIVE: To increase familiarity with the alphabet and improve spelling ability.

MATERIALS NEEDED: Paper, pencil, and dictionary (or thesaurus) for each student.

DESCRIPTION: Each player writes down THREE WORDS of 4 to 8 letters each. Then, each, in turn, calls out 1 letter, and everyone crosses out that letter everywhere it appears in each of his words. The first person with all THREE WORDS completely eliminated is the winner.

ADAPTATION: This game can also be played using numbers instead of words. Each student would write down THREE NUMBERS instead of THREE WORDS. Each number would consist of 4 to 8 digits and the students would, in turn, call out numbers instead of letters.

SUGGESTIONS: I usually have the student call out a letter accompanied by a word that begins with that letter, in order to avoid confusion. For example:

> **G**, as in **G**eorge; **J**, as in **J**ohn; **E**, as in **E**lephant; **I**, as in **I**ntelligent

Occasionally, we restrict the THREE WORDS to a specific category, such as animals, classroom objects, or cities. This tends to expand vocabulary in the category chosen. The use of dictionaries (or thesauruses) enables students to expand their vocabulary even more.

56. SUPER SECRETARY

L, W

level: intermediate
optimal group size: unlimited

OBJECTIVE: To strengthen vocabulary, spelling, syntax and memory ability.

MATERIALS NEEDED: Five to 10 pieces of chalk and an equal number of sections of blackboard.

DESCRIPTION: The class is divided into equal teams of 5 to 7 players each. The first player from each team goes to the blackboard and writes the sentence dictated by the teacher. The game ends when all players have had a turn at the board.

Scoring: (a) A correct sentence is worth 5 points.
Subtract 1 point for each error (to a maximum of 5 points).

OR

(b) Only a correct sentence gains 1 point.
No points are awarded if errors exist.

SUGGESTION: To make it more challenging, I read the sentence **only once.** This forces students to listen very attentively and to try to remember the entire sentence. I watch for errors in syntax, spelling, and punctuation.

57. LETTERGORY

L, S

level: intermediate
optimal group size: unlimited

OBJECTIVE: To review vocabulary and parts of speech.

MATERIALS NEEDED: None.

DESCRIPTION: The group is divided into 2 equal teams. The teacher calls out a part of speech and a letter. The first person to call out a word that begins with that letter and is that part of speech wins 1 point for his team. For example:

Teacher:	Verb. K.	Student:	Kiss.
Teacher:	Noun. W.	Student:	Wagon.
Teacher:	Preposition. N.	Student:	Near.
Teacher:	Adjective. E.	Student:	Exciting.

SUGGESTIONS: I find that there is less confusion if the part of speech is named *before* the letter. If the letter is named first, some students will be tempted to take some "shots in the dark" before they hear the part of speech.

Also, to avoid pandemonium, the competition should be limited to 2 players at a time (one from each team).

58. OPPOSITES

L, S, R

level: intermediate
optimal group size: 10

OBJECTIVE: To reinforce and expand vocabulary, especially adjectives, adverbs and verbs, and their opposites.

MATERIALS NEEDED: A deck of flashcards, each with either an adjective, adverb, or verb on it. Each word used must have an opposite, but its opposite isn't written on the card. For example:

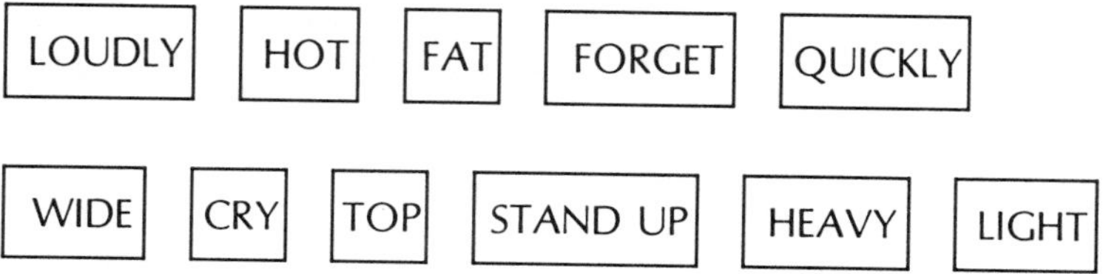

DESCRIPTION: The group is divided into 2 teams (A and B). The first person on Team A chooses a word and challenges the first person on Team B to give the opposite in a sentence. Then B1 challenges A1, and so on. For example:

A1: "My father is FAT." . . . B1: "My father is THIN."
B1: "This book is LIGHT." . . . A1: "This book is HEAVY."
A2: "I CRY when I'm sad." . . . B2: "I LAUGH when I'm sad."
B2: "She talks LOUDLY." . . . A2: "I don't know!"

Scoring: 1 point for a correct challenge.
1 point for a correct opposite.
2 points if you know the opposite that your opponent doesn't.

SUGGESTION: If the correct answer isn't known, it is revealed by the teacher.

59. RHYME WHIRL

R, W

level: intermediate
optimal group size: 20

OBJECTIVE: To expand vocabulary, specifically words that rhyme.

MATERIALS NEEDED: Dictionaries and the Rhyme Disc (2 concentric discs, fastenend in the centre, able to spin independently of each other). On the outside disc, various consonant blends are written around the perimeter. On the inside disc, rhyme endings are written around the perimeter. For example:

bl/end, br/ing, bl/ack, cl/ean, cr/op, dr/eam, scr/ap, pl/ease, tr/ue, pr/oud, pr/ice, str/ong, sw/ing, sl/eep, fr/om.

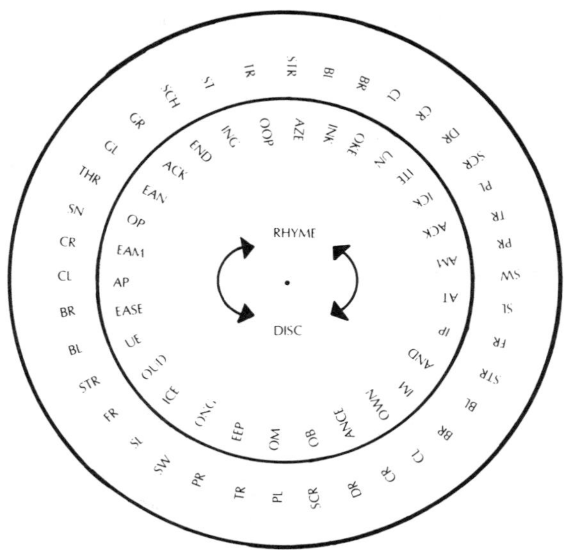

DESCRIPTION: Students, in turn, spin the Rhyme Disc and find a combination of a consonant blend and a rhyme ending that forms a legitimate word. When a student has found a workable combination, he returns to his desk and, with the help of a dictionary, looks for as many words as he can find that rhyme with his word. In the unlikely event that a student spins the Rhyme Disc and no word can be formed, he spins again until he has a word to work with. For example:

CL + EAN = CLEAN bean, mean, lean, seen, scene, machine . . .

(Rhyme, not spelling, is important.)

SUGGESTIONS: I have my slower students spin first so they have more time to find their rhyming words.

Also, to ensure that meaningful learning is taking place, I have my students include a short definition with each word they find.

60. TIC-TAC-TENSE

L, S, R

level: intermediate
optimal group size: 20

OBJECTIVE: To review various verb tenses.

MATERIALS NEEDED: Overhead projector, or grid (see below) drawn on the blackboard.

today	last night	next year
two weeks ago	next month	this morning
this evening	yesterday	tomorrow afternoon

DESCRIPTION: The group is divided into 2 teams (Team X and Team O). One person from Team X chooses a position on the grid and uses that time expression in a sentence in the appropriate tense. For example:

> *Two weeks ago,* I broke my leg.
>
> *Next year,* I'm going to visit my cousins in Texas.

A correct response gives that position to your team. If an error is made, the position remains vacant and the turn goes to the opposing team. The teams alternate turns trying to get 3 positions in a row (horizontally, vertically, or diagonally) to win.

61. WHAT'S MY LINE?

L, S

level: intermediate
optimal group size: unlimited

OBJECTIVE: To give students practice in asking questions requiring YES/NO answers.

MATERIALS NEEDED: None.

DESCRIPTION: The class tries to guess the occupation (real or fictitious) of the challenger. Only questions requiring YES/NO answers may be posed by the guessers. For example:

Do you work with machines?
Do you wear a uniform?
Can a child do your job?
Do other people work with you?
Are you a supervisor?

SUGGESTION: I usually limit the number of questions asked to half the number of students in the group, or 20. If the occupation hasn't been guessed by then, it is revealed and a new challenger takes his turn.

62. LOST AND FOUND

L, S

level: intermediate
optimal group size: unlimited

OBJECTIVE: To give students practice in describing objects.

MATERIALS NEEDED: Students' pens, rulers, notebooks, combs, and other personal (but inexpensive and durable) objects.

DESCRIPTION: One-half of the group places 2 (or more) objects onto a desk in the centre of the room. They then take turns describing their possessions to the others, who try to locate the items described and return them to their rightful owners.

When the desk is cleared of all objects, the roles are reversed.

3. CATEGORIES

R, W

level: intermediate
optimal group size: unlimited

OBJECTIVE: To expand students' vocabulary.

MATERIALS NEEDED: Pen, paper, and dictionary for each student. A grid in which there are 5 different letters across the top and 5 categories down the left side. The 5 letters can constitute a word, if you prefer.

Example:

	B	L	A	C	K
Colours				*crimson*	
Animals		*llama*			
Foods					*kohlrabi*
Countries	*Burma*				
Furniture			*armchair*		

Other possible categories include: *drinks, song titles, cities, adjectives, verbs, languages, names, car parts, sports, professions* and *athletes*.

DESCRIPTION: Students are presented with the grid and are challenged (individually, or in teams of 3 to 5 players) to find a word for each category which begins with each letter. In the example above, for instance, students must find the names of COLOURS that begin with the letters B, L, A, C, and K. They must also find the names of ANIMALS, FOODS, COUNTRIES and FURNITURE that begin with the letters B, L, A, C, and K.

SUGGESTIONS: I encourage my students to be adventurous and to look for unusual words (for example, "burgundy" instead of "blue"). This game is best played non-competitively. I simply ask: "Who has an interesting word for a colour that begins with the letter 'B'?"

64. MYSTERY PERSON

L

level: intermediate
optimal group size: unlimited

OBJECTIVE: To develop critical listening skills.

MATERIALS NEEDED: None.

DESCRIPTION: The teacher describes an unnamed student to the class, while they try to guess his identity. Physical characteristics, clothing, personal traits, etc, can all be used in the description.

SUGGESTIONS: I have found that breaking the class up into teams of 4 or 5 players each allows students to interact and confer with one another before guessing. To encourage precision, I impose a penalty of minus 2 for each wrong guess, while a correct guess is worth 5 points. Occasionally, to test students' memories, I have played MYSTERY PERSON with their heads down and their eyes closed. This forces them to listen more carefully and to recall a person's appearance from memory instead of looking around to see who fits the description.

65. PAIRED LETTERS

R, W

level: intermediate
optimal group size: unlimited

OBJECTIVE: To expand vocabulary and reinforce spelling ability.

MATERIALS NEEDED: Pen, paper, and dictionary for each student. Overhead projector or blackboard.

DESCRIPTION: Students are shown the following grid, and the person who creates the greatest number of words by combining PAIRED LETTERS is the winner.

li	bi	ea	so	ye
at	yi	ow	ll	ki
ti	kn	ng	fe	bl
op	ck	st	ro	me
ca	in	si	ar	lo

Here are a few words that can be formed by combining PAIRED LETTERS from this grid:

liar	stop
strong	star
yellow	yell
rock	sill
know	feat
fellow	fear

SUGGESTIONS: I usually impose a time limit of 5 minutes. When I first introduce this game to a class, I let them work with a partner to ease them into it. To encourage the formation of longer words, I often count 2 points for a four-letter word, 4 points for a six-letter word, 8 points for an eight-letter word, 16 points for a ten-letter word, and so on, doubling the points for each additional pair of letters.

To make your own grid, simply break up words of 4, 6, 8 and 10 letters and scatter the PAIRED LETTERS over the grid.

66. INTERROGATION

L, S, R, W

level: intermediate
optimal group size: unlimited

OBJECTIVE: To strengthen the ability to ask questions.

MATERIALS NEEDED: Pen and paper for each student.

DESCRIPTION: The class is divided into teams of 5 to 7 players each. The first player on each team composes a number of questions equal to the number of players on his team, excluding himself. The questions should relate to a particular subject. He then whispers one question to each member of his team and writes down their responses. Then he collates the answers and writes the complete story. When he has finished, he relates the story to the class. Then, the other players on his team take turns composing and whispering questions, and finally writing stories.

Note: Each player hears only the question posed to him and none of the answers of the others. For example:

S1: "What do you want?" — S2: "I want a car."
S1: "Why do you want it?" — S3: "Because it's delicious."
S1: "What will you do with it?" — S4: "I'll sleep with it."
S1: "Where will you put it?" — S5: "I'll put it in the bathtub."
S1: "How much does it cost?" — S6: "It costs a million dollars."
S1: "What will you do with it after that?" — S7: "I'll eat it."

67. WAITER/WAITRESS

L, W

level: intermediate
optimal group size: 10

OBJECTIVE: To develop listening skills.

MATERIALS NEEDED: A pen and paper for each student, and one restaurant menu.

DESCRIPTION: Students record the teacher's order as he chooses from the menu. The person with the most complete and accurate list dictates his order to the group on the next round. For example:

> "I'll have a shrimp cocktail to start. Then the chicken vegetable soup and the New York cut steak, medium-rare, with a baked potato instead of French fries and a chef's salad with the house dressing. For dessert, I'd like tea and rice pudding, please."

,UGGESTION: With students of legal age, I often order alcoholic beverages with my meal, to familiarize them with the names of various drinks.

68. PUZZLE WORDS

R, W

level: intermediate
optimal group size: unlimited

OBJECTIVE: To develop vocabulary.

MATERIALS NEEDED: Pen and paper for each student. Dictionaries may prove helpful.

DESCRIPTION: Each student draws a square and divides it into 9 squares. He then chooses a nine-letter word and arranges it in the squares **so that consecutive letters touch one another.** Each letter of the word can be used only once, of course. They then challenge one another to discover their PUZZLE WORDS.

Examples: (Arrows are only to clarify the examples.)

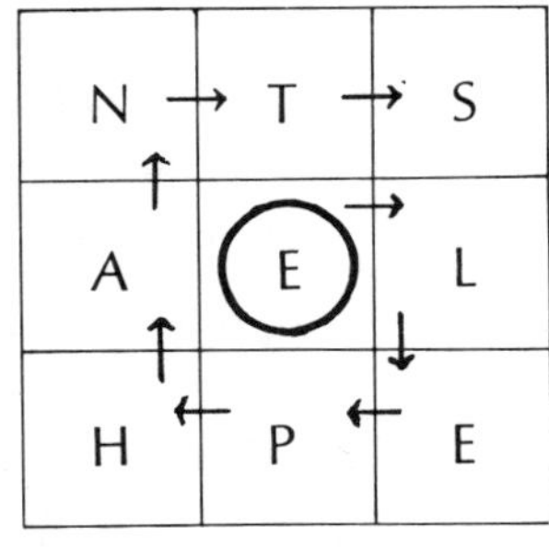

(elephants)

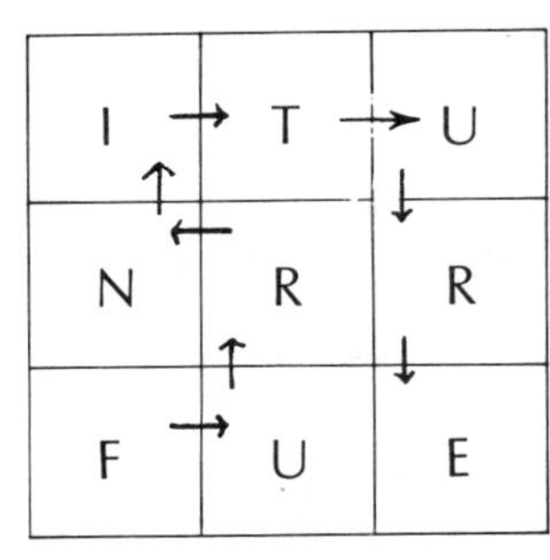

(furniture)

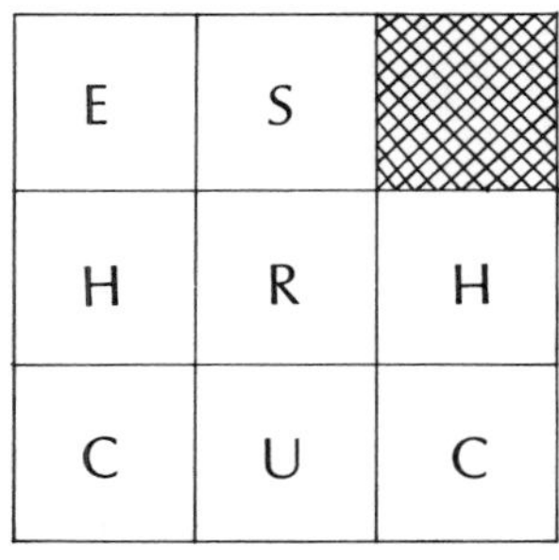

(churches)

(You're on your own!)

SUGGESTIONS: I have my students circle the first letter for the first challenge, to ease their opponents into the game.

The solution isn't written beneath the challenge, nor are the arrows drawn in when students play the game. I've done it in the examples merely to show you some arrangements.

When I introduce this game to a class for the first time, I display several PUZZLE WORDS on the overhead or blackboard and challenge the entire class to solve them. I then invite an individual to show the class his solution to one of the PUZZLE WORDS. Then, students are ready to create their own and challenge one another.

69. QUESTIONS AND ANSWERS

L, S

level: intermediate
optimal group size: unlimited

OBJECTIVE: To give students practice asking and answering questions.

MATERIALS NEEDED: None.

DESCRIPTION: The class is divided into 2 teams (A and B). Players take turns composing and answering WHO, WHEN, WHERE, WHY and HOW questions. One point for a grammatically correct question, and 1 for a grammatically correct answer.

For example:

A1:	"**Where** did Jack go last night?"	(1 point)
B1:	"He went to the movies."	(1 point)
B2:	"**How** are you going to France?"	(1 point)
A2:	"I'm going by ship."	(1 point)
A3:	"**What** did you eat for supper last night?"	(1 point)
B3:	"I eated pizza for supper."	(*no* point)
B4:	"**Why** said you 'goodbye' to me?"	(*no* point)
A4:	"I said 'goodbye' because I was leaving."	(1 point)

SUGGESTIONS: The teacher is the judge and awards points. Errors should be corrected immediately, either by a student or by the teacher if no one knows how to correct the error(s).

70. EXAGGERATION

R, W

level: intermediate
optimal group size: unlimited

OBJECTIVE: To reinforce the use of SO + $\frac{\text{ADJECTIVE}}{\text{ADVERB}}$ + THAT, and and SUCH + (A/AN) + ADJECTIVE + NOUN + THAT.

MATERIALS NEEDED: Rough paper and pencil for each student, plus two sheets of good paper (or cardboard salvaged from boxes of copy paper).

DESCRIPTION: The teacher provides several humorous examples and gives the students a free rein (or almost free) to create several of their own. For example:

My brother is **so stupid that** he studied for his blood test.

He talks **so slowly that** people are finished listening before he's finished speaking.

She has **such a loud voice that** she never pays for long-distance phone calls.

He has **such big ears that** on windy days he has to tuck them under his belt to keep from flying away.

The teacher helps where needed and chooses each student's best 2 sentences to be re-copied on the good paper and fastened to the walls or ceiling for display.

Note: Every time I do this with my students, they invariably invite other students into our room to read their hilarious creations. I usually leave them up for about 2 weeks and I find that students have committed all of them to memory because they enjoyed them so much.

71. MAKE A SENTENCE

R, L, S

level: intermediate
optimal group size: 10

OBJECTIVE: To review and reinforce the use of problematic words and expressions.

MATERIALS NEEDED: At least 30 flashcards with either a noun, verb, conjunction, adverb, preposition, adjective, or expression on each.

DESCRIPTION: The pile of cards is inverted. Students sit around the inverted pile of cards and each, in turn, takes one and uses the word(s) on it in a sentence or two to show the meaning. For example:

UNLESS	You can't go out **unless** you have finished your homework.
DIFFERENT FROM	Your hair is **different from** mine. Yours is long and mine is short.
NEVER	I **never** drive after drinking alcohol.
FEWER	John has two pencils and Carol has three. John has **fewer** pencils than Carol.

I USED TO — **I used to** smoke, but I stopped four years ago.

(You would, of course, choose words and expressions which require review and reinforcing for your students.)

Scoring: 2 points for a perfect sentence.
1 point for a good sentence with few errors.
Zero for nonsense.

SUGGESTION: I give any student 1 point if he can correct the error(s) in the previous student's sentence(s). This encourages them all to listen carefully to one another's sentences.

72. ALPHABETICAL ADJECTIVES

W, L, S

level: intermediate
optimal group size: unlimited

OBJECTIVE: To expand vocabulary (specifically, adjectives).

MATERIALS NEEDED: Blackboard, dictionary, pen and paper.

DESCRIPTION: The teacher writes a short sentence on the blackboard using an adjective which begins with the letter "a." The adjective is underlined. Challenge the students to rewrite the sentence, replacing the adjective with others which begin with consecutive letters of the alphabet. For example:

Teacher: "I saw an _ancient_ house."

Student 1: "I saw a _beautiful_ house."
"I saw a _cheap_ house."
"I saw a _drab_ house."

Student 2: "I saw a _big_ house."
"I saw a _classy_ house."
"I saw a _dumpy_ house."

Student 3: "I saw a boxy house."
"I saw a creepy house."
"I saw a dreary house."

SUGGESTION: I encourage students to read their most interesting and unusual sentences to the class and they explain those that require clarification.

73. LETTER GETTER

L, S

level: intermediate
optimal group size: 20

OBJECTIVE: To expand vocabulary.

MATERIALS NEEDED: A set of alphabet flashcards.

DESCRIPTION: Four equal teams are formed. The teacher calls out a category (such as animal, person, sport, etc.) and holds up a random letter. The first team to call out a word which fits the category and starts with that letter wins that letter. The team with the most letters at the end of the game is the winner.

SUGGESTION: For boisterous classes, I confine the competition to one member of each team at a time. For example, among teams A, B, C, and D, players A1, B1, C1, and D1 are the only ones who are permitted to respond. During the next round, A2, B2, C2, and D2 compete for the letter, while the others watch and listen quietly awaiting their turns.

74. SUITABLE ADJECTIVES

R, L, S

level: intermediate
optimal group size: 20

OBJECTIVE: To expand vocabulary.

MATERIALS NEEDED: A list of nouns on the overhead or blackboard.

DESCRIPTION: The group is divided into 2 teams – Team A and Team B. The first player of Team A chooses a noun from the list and uses a suitable adjective to describe it. The first player on Team B uses another adjective to modify the same noun, and each player, in turn, tries to use a suitable adjective to qualify the same noun. When one player repeats a previously used adjective, uses an unsuitable adjective (such as a "delicious house"), or cannot think of an original suitable adjective, the other team gains a point. A new round is begun by the losing team.

75. WHAT'S MY RHYME?

L, S

level: intermediate
optimal group size: unlimited

OBJECTIVE: To develop vocabulary.

MATERIALS NEEDED: Pen and paper.

DESCRIPTION: The class is divided into 5 equal teams. The first Team (Team A) decides on a word (for example, KNIT), and writes it down on the paper. They then challenge the other teams to guess their word by saying: "We have a word that rhymes with 'sit'. What is it?"

The other teams (B, C, D, and E) take turns guessing the mystery word by defining it, but not naming it. For example:

B: "Is it a violent action?"
A: "No, it isn't hit."

C: "Is it like a glove?"
A: "No, it isn't mitt."

D: "Is it the past form of LIGHT?"
A: "No, it isn't lit."

E: "Is it how you make a sweater?"
A: "Yes, it is knit."

One point is scored by the team who guesses correctly. If the word isn't guessed within a pre-determined time limit (for example, 2 minutes), the challenging team wins a point.

76. TIC-TAC-FREQUENCY

L, S, R

level: intermediate
optimal group size: 20

OBJECTIVE: To review various adverbs of frequency.

MATERIALS NEEDED: The following grid on the blackboard or overhead.

sometimes	often	always
generally	never	seldom
occasionally	rarely	usually

DESCRIPTION: The group is divided into 2 teams (Team X and Team O). One player from Team X chooses a position on the grid and uses the expression (adverb of frequency) in that space in an appropriate sentence. For example:

"I **sometimes** walk to school."

If he is correct, Team X occupies that position. If he makes a mistake, the space remains vacant and Team O can try for any vacant position which will help them gain 3 positions in a row (vertically, horizontally, or diagonally) to win.

77. MY/MINE

L, S

level: intermediate
optimal group size: unlimited

OBJECTIVE: To reinforce the use of possessive adjectives and possessive pronouns.

MATERIALS NEEDED: None.

DESCRIPTION: The class is divided into 2 teams (A and B). The first student on Team A uses a possessive adjective in a sentence to which the first student on Team B must respond using the corresponding possessive pronoun. For example:

A1: "**My** car is brown."
B1: "**Mine** is green.

Then B1 challenges A1 in return, and so on down the ranks.

B1: "**Her** father is old."
A1: "**Hers** is young."

A2: "**Our** house is white."
B2: "**Ours** is white, too."

B2: "**His** hair is long."
A2: "**His** is short."

A mistake costs your team a point.

78. DEAFMAN

L, S

level: intermediate
optimal group size: unlimited

OBJECTIVE: To give students practice in using indirect/reported speech.

MATERIALS NEEDED: None.

DESCRIPTION: Students are grouped in 3s. The first asks a question or makes a statement. The second, pretending not to have heard, asks the third what has been said. The third reports what has been said.

Examples:
Student A: "It's cold outside."
Student B: "What did he say?"
Student C: "He said that it was cold outside."

Student C: "Where did you go last night?"
Student A: "What did she ask you?"
Student B: "She asked where I went/had gone last night."

Student B: "My brother is fifteen years old."
Student C: "What did he say?"
Student A: "He said that his brother was fifteen years old."

SUGGESTION: I always have the roles alternated so that everyone has the chance to play all parts. The last person starts the next round.

79. SENTENCE RELAY

R, W

level: intermediate
optimal group size: unlimited

OBJECTIVE: To encourage proper sentence construction (syntax).

MATERIALS NEEDED: Several pieces of chalk and an equal number of sections of blackboard.

DESCRIPTION: The class is divided into teams of 5 to 7 players each. On a signal from the teacher, the first player of each team goes to the board and writes a word (any word) on the board. He then hands the chalk to the second member of his team who writes another word in front of, or behind, the first word. Every other player, in turn, adds a word and the last member of each team must complete the sentence including punctuation. There is to be no conferring among team members. The number of words in each team's sentence will equal the number of players on that team. For example:

Team A: (7 players)

	It	is	very	hot	today,	isn't	it?
Player #	3	4	5	1	2	6	7

Team B: (6 players)

	We	went	to	the	movies	yesterday.
Player #	1	2	3	4	5	6

Team C: (5 players)

	I	watch	television	every	night.
Player #	3	2	1	4	5

Team D: (6 players)

	John	visited	Mary	Jones	last	week.
Player #	3	4	5	6	1	2

Team E: (7 players)

	Did	your	old	uncle	come	from	Edmonton?
Player #	1	2	3	4	5	6	7

Team F: (6 players)

	My sister was born in Toronto.
Player #	6 5 4 3 2 1

SUGGESTION: After all sentences are read (and corrected as required), the last player on each team goes to the board first in the next round. This way, everybody gets an equal opportunity to play each role.

80. WHAT AM I?

L, S, R, W

level: intermediate
optimal group size: unlimited

OBJECTIVE: To develop critical listening and description skills.

MATERIALS NEEDED: Pen and paper for each student.

DESCRIPTION: Students create riddles and take turns posing them to the others. For example:

Student 1: "I am as flat as the floor, made of wood, and I separate rooms. WHAT AM I?"
(Solution: A door.)

Student 2: "I am white, round, and in the sky. WHAT AM I?"
(Solution: The moon.)

Student 3: "I am soft wool (or nylon) and I cover the floor. WHAT AM I?"
(Solution: A carpet.)

The person who guesses correctly can take his turn at challenging the group.

SUGGESTION: Having students write down, then read, their riddles speeds up the game and reduces arguments about what was said.

81. VERB AND PREPOSITION/ADVERB

R, S

level: intermediate
optimal group size: 20

OBJECTIVE: To review two-word verbs.

MATERIALS NEEDED: A VERB AND PREPOSITION/ADVERB pointer or VERB AND PREPOSITION/ADVERB cards in piles.

The following verbs are printed, once each, around the VERB circle (or on VERB cards): look, take, put, pick, light, throw, turn, clean, rub, pull, push, try, give, call, fix, write, find, open, close, knock, dry, lift, zip, switch, tear, and wipe. The following prepositions/adverbs are printed around the PREPOSITION/ADVERB circle (or on PREPOSITION/ADVERB cards). Each preposition/adverb is repeated 3 times: in, out, at, off, on, up, down, away, and back.

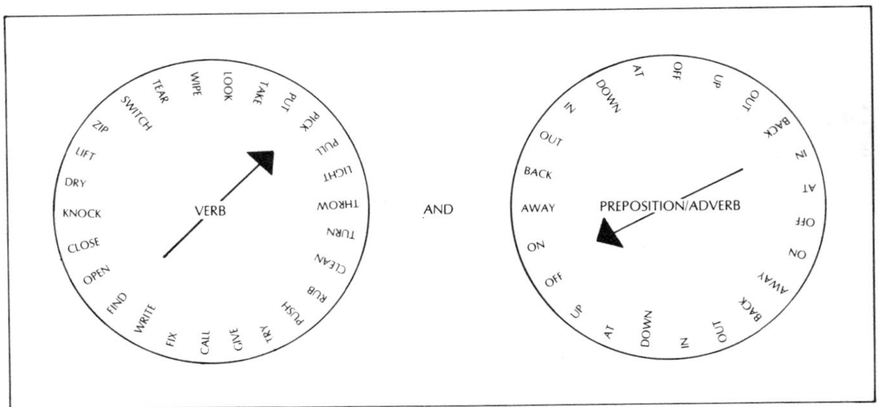

OR

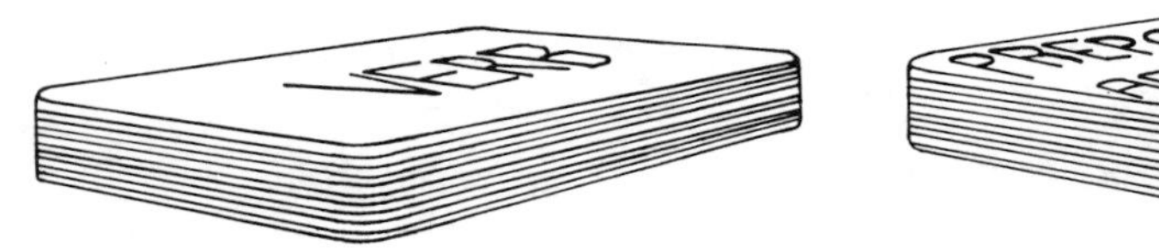

DESCRIPTION: Students take turns spinning both pointers (or picking a card from each pile) for a VERB and a PREPOSITION/ADVERB. For 1 point, he must tell whether the combination is compatible ("Yes" or "No").

If it **is** compatible, a second point can be won by using a form of the combination in a sentence (or two) to show meaning. For example:

Student 1:	TURN + DOWN . . .	Yes. (1 point) Please **turn down** your stereo. It's too loud. (2nd point)
Student 2:	FIND + AWAY . . .	No. (1 point)
Student 3:	LIFT + AT . . .	No. (1 point)
Student 4:	TEAR + OFF . . .	Yes. (1 point) Be sure to **tear off** the price tag before you give the gift. (2nd point)
Student 5:	GIVE + AWAY . . .	Yes. (1 point) I **gave away** my old coat to a poor family. (2nd point)

82. TWO-WORD VERBS

R, L, S

level: intermediate
optimal group size: 10

OBJECTIVE: To review and reinforce two-word verbs.

MATERIALS NEEDED: Cards with a two-word verb on each. Each verb is written once on 3 separate cards.

Example: | TAKE OFF | TURN ON | LIFT UP | PUT DOWN |

DESCRIPTION: The cards are placed face-down in a pile. Students sit around the inverted pile of cards, and each one takes a card in turn. The card is kept if 2 correct sentences are made using a form of the verb on it. For example:

I'm **taking off** my shoes. I'm **taking** them **off.**

If a mistake is made, the card is returned to the bottom of the pile.

The winner is the first person to accumulate 3 identical cards or 10 cards in total. Here are some examples of two-word verbs:

turn off, on, back, over, down, up, away
lift up, off
zip up, down
put on, down, away, off, back, out
clean off, up, out
give back, up, away, out
take off, out, away, in, back, down, up

83. GRAMMAR RELAY

L, W, R

level: intermediate
optimal group size: unlimited

OBJECTIVE: To review parts of speech and construct sentences using them.

MATERIALS NEEDED: Five pens and 5 sheets of paper. Several sentences written by the teacher.

DESCRIPTION: The class is divided into five equal teams. The first player on each team has the pen and paper. The teacher chooses one sentence, for example, "George parks in his garage." He then calls out each part of speech, one at a time, as each player writes down an example. The first player writes down an example of the first part of speech, and passes the paper to the second player on his team, who writes an example of the second part of speech named, and so on down the ranks until the sentence is complete. The last player puts the appropriate punctuation in and reads his team's sentence to the class. One team point is won for a grammatically correct sentence. The last player starts the next round.

Here are some sample sentences:

Teacher: (1) PROPER NOUN (2) VERB (3) PREPOSITION (4) ADJECTIVE (5) NOUN (6) PUNCTUATION

Team A's sentence: Jack climbed into old clothes.
Team B's sentence: Montreal is in western Quebec.
Team C's sentence: Carol slept in dirty pyjamas.
Team D's sentence: King John is on his throne.
Team E's sentence: Mr. Carson went to his cottage.
Team F's sentence: Susan eats at her table.
Team G's sentence: Barry rode on his new bike.

Teacher: (1) QUESTION WORD (2) AUXILIARY VERB (3) PRONOUN (4) VERB (5) NOUN (6) PUNCTUATION

Team A's sentence: Where does he eat lunch?
Team B's sentence: How do you say 'hello'?
Team C's sentence: Why is she watching television?
Team D's sentence: Whom is she seeing, John?
Team E's sentence: When did you drink tea?
Team F's sentence: Where did you go yesterday?
Team G's sentence: What did you say, Sharon?

SUGGESTION: When I introduce this game for the first time, I have the students go to the board, in turn, and write their words on the board for all to see. This enables them to learn from one another since all attempts are visible and can be analyzed.

4. NEWSCAST

L, S, R, W

levels: intermediate and advanced
optimal group size: 10

OBJECTIVE: To develop critical listening skills.

MATERIALS NEEDED: Short, student-written stories on any topic.

DESCRIPTION: The students in the group take turns reading their stories to the others and, when finished, ask WHO, WHEN, WHERE, WHY and WHAT HAPPENED questions of the group.

SUGGESTIONS: A class of 40 students could be broken up into 4 groups of 10 for greater individual involvement. Also, I have found that short narratives about an interesting event in their lives work best since, being personal, interest is naturally high.

85. CHAIN STORIES

L, S

levels: intermediate and advanced
optimal group size: 10

OBJECTIVE: To give students practice in following and adding to a story line. This aids comprehension and adds to oral creativity and expression.

MATERIALS NEEDED: None.

DESCRIPTION: The teacher begins a story (using the verb tenses and vocabulary most appropriate for the capabilities of the students) and randomly names students to continue the story in turn. For example:

> Teacher – "Several years ago, as I was walking home from the theatre, I saw a large, white dog . . .
> Robert, would you like to continue the story?"
>
> Robert – "It was trying to cross the street from the other side, but the traffic was too heavy. It started to cross several times, but ran back, afraid of the cars . . ."
>
> Teacher – "Then what happened, Susan?"

Susan – "I yelled to it to sit and it sat down immediately on the curb. I crossed the street when it was safe, and patted it gently, while I spoke softly to it . . ."

Teacher – "Jack, please continue."

Jack – "As I spoke and patted it, it calmed down and began to lick my hand. When the traffic became lighter, I led it across the street . . ."

Teacher – "What happened next, Grace?"

86. WORDS WITHIN

R, W

levels: intermediate and advanced
optimal group size: unlimited

OBJECTIVE: To develop vocabulary.

MATERIALS NEEDED: Blackboard or overhead projector, dictionaries, paper and pencil.

DESCRIPTION: The teacher challenges the group to make as many words as they can from the letters of a key word, for example:

UNFORGETTABLE: Some of the the words that they can form are: table, forge, gable, glean, fortune, fort, etc.

Rules:
1. New words must have at least 4 letters.
2. Proper nouns are not acceptable.
3. Five-minute time limit.

SUGGESTION: I encourage my students to use their dictionaries to further increase vocabulary development.

87. PREDICAMENTS

L, S

levels: intermediate and advanced
optimal group size: unlimited

OBJECTIVE: To review the First and Second Conditional Tenses.

MATERIALS NEEDED: None.

DESCRIPTION: One student leaves the room while the others decide on a predicament such as: being caught asleep in class. When the student returns, he asks others, in turn, "What would **you** do?" (or "What would **you** have done?" if the Second Conditional Tense is being reviewed). Each response must be original and brief, giving very little away. For example:

S2: I would say "I'm sorry."

S3: I would leave the room.

S4: I would go home and go to sleep.

S5: I would make up an excuse.

S6: I would yawn and apologize.

S7: I would stretch and ask if I could splash some cold water on my face.

S8: I would quickly state that it wasn't because the lesson was boring.

The student tries to guess what the predicament was. Here are a few more predicaments that have worked well with my classes:

The big, strong, and rude taxi driver claims that you gave him a ten-dollar bill, not a twenty.

A very attractive person has accidentally tapped your car at a stoplight.

At a very posh restaurant, the waiter accidentally drops your salad in your lap.

A man in the crowded elevator has lit up a cigarette and the smoke is bothering you.

You are driving alone down a dark, lonely road and a man tries to flag you down.

88. FINISH IT!

L, S, R, W

levels: intermediate and advanced
optimal group size: unlimited

OBJECTIVE: To learn and practise similes.

MATERIALS NEEDED: Pen and paper.

DESCRIPTION: Students are paired off and each writes down and completes 10 similes (5 **as** and 5 **like**). They then challenge each other to complete orally each other's similes exactly as they have done. For example:

as light as . . .	he laughs like . . .
as juicy as . . .	she runs like . . .
as funny as . . .	we cried like . . .
as happy as . . .	he bled like . . .
as tall as . . .	it flew like . . .
as fast as . . .	he yelled like . . .
as brightly as . . .	she kisses like . . .
as loudly as . . .	he swims like . . .
as softly as . . .	she drives like . . .
as carefully as . . .	it rained like . . .

Scoring: One point is awarded for each duplication. The more interesting similes can be read to the class.

89. HOW MANY WORDS?

L, S, R, W

levels: intermediate and advanced
optimal group size: unlimited

OBJECTIVE: To develop vocabulary.

MATERIALS NEEDED: Dictionaries, pen and paper.

DESCRIPTION: Divide the class into 5 teams. Assign a number of questions: HOW MANY WORDS can you find . . .

that rhyme with "ball"?
that mean the same as "heavy"?
that start with "bl"?
that describe temperature?
that are names of insects?
that mean the opposite of "strong"?
that end in "ion"?
that are colours?

The team with the most words wins a point for that question.

90. MISFITS

L, W

levels: intermediate and advanced
optimal group size: unlimited

OBJECTIVE: To review vocabulary.

MATERIALS NEEDED: Dictionaries, pen and paper.

DESCRIPTION: The teacher reads several four-word sets. Three of the four words are related, while the fourth is not. The students try to write down the misfits. One point for each correct misfit. Here are some possible categories: musical instruments; appliances; religions; wild animals; vegetables; grammatical terms; sports; tools; fruits; car parts; furniture; writing tools; materials; languages. (Students are not told what the category is.) For example:

trombone, chair, saxophone, piano

lion, tiger, elephant, football

verb, noun, fork, adjective

apple, screwdriver, wrench, hammer

SUGGESTION: Dictionaries will prove very helpful if the game is played with more advanced vocabulary written on paper or the overhead projector.

91. BIOGRAPHY

R, L, S

levels: intermediate and advanced
optimal group size: unlimited

OBJECTIVE: To give students practice asking and answering questions in various tenses.

MATERIALS NEEDED: Biographies of several famous people on paper, the blackboard or overhead projector. (Most accounts in encyclopedias are quite adequate.)

DESCRIPTION: The class is divided into 2 teams (A and B). Details of a famous person's career and life are presented to the students. Members of each team take turns asking and answering questions about that person. Two points for a correct question and 1 for a correct answer. For example:

A1: "Where was X born?"
B1: "He was born in Paris, France."

B2: "When did he graduate from Y college?"
A2: "He graduated in 1926."

A3: "How did he get from Lyons to Marseilles?"
B3: "He went by train."

B4: "What did he do in 1929?"
A4: "He got married."

A5: "Who influenced his life the most?"
B5: "His sister did."

B6: "Where was he in 1932?"
A6: "He was in England."

SUGGESTION: If time permits, open-ended questions which involve the deductive/inductive process could be introduced. For example: "How do you think he would feel about nuclear disarmament if he were alive today?"

92. ALPHABET

W

levels: intermediate and advanced
optimal group size: unlimited

OBJECTIVE: To expand and develop vocabulary.

MATERIALS NEEDED: Pencil and paper.

DESCRIPTION: A category is presented (animals, countries, names of cars, verbs, abstract nouns, etc) and the first student to compile a list of 26 words beginning with consecutive letters of the alphabet is the winner, or the team with the most words at the end of the allotted time wins.

SUGGESTION: Students could be permitted to work in teams of 4 or 5 to facilitate and expedite the task.

93. OUT

R, W

levels: intermediate and advanced
optimal group size: 10

OBJECTIVE: To review vocabulary and reinforce spelling ability.

MATERIALS NEEDED: Blackboard.

DESCRIPTION: The first player thinks of a word (of more than 3 letters) and says the first letter which the teacher writes on the board. The second player thinks of a word (again, consisting of more than 3 letters) which begins with that letter, and gives the second letter of his word which is added to the letter already on the board. The third player thinks of a word (more than 3 letters) that begins with the 2 letters on the board and gives its third letter. Each successive player, in turn, adds a letter which he hopes will *continue*, but *not complete* a word. Each time you complete a word, you gain 1 letter of OUT and are on your way out. If you suspect that the player before you doesn't have a legitimate word in mind, you can challenge him by asking, "What's your word?" If he was bluffing and doesn't have a word in mind, he gains a letter of OUT. If he does have a legitimate word, the challenger gains a letter of OUT. When an individual has all 3 letters of OUT, he is, indeed, out.

The next round is begun by the player who gained a letter of OUT in the last round.

Note: Only words of more than 3 letters count as words; otherwise words of 1, 2, or 3 letters would drastically shorten the game.

For more advanced classes, I raise the quota to 4 or more letters in order to get more interesting words.

Here are a few sample rounds:

1st player thinks of **P**OOL and says **P**.

2nd player thinks of P**L**ACE and says **L**.

3rd player thinks of PL**A**NE and says **A**.

4th player thinks of PLA**N**T and says **N**. But PLAN is a word of more than 3 letters, so the 4th player gets the O of OUT, since he completed a word, and is one third of his way out.

Next Round: (Begun by the player who got a letter of OUT in the last round.)

4th player thinks of **T**HREE and says **T**.

5th player thinks of T**R**EE and says **R**.

6th player thinks of TR**I**M and says **I**.

7th player thinks of TRI**C**K and says **C**.

8th player thinks of TRIC**K** but knows that if he says **K**, he will have completed a word, so he tries to think of any other letter that will continue but not complete a word. Failing that, he decides to bluff and adds **L**.

9th player can't think of a word that starts off with TRICL, so he challenges the 8th player who admits that he has no word in mind. The 8th player gets the O of OUT, and starts the next round.

94. WORD EXPLOSION

R, W

levels: intermediate and advanced
optimal group size: unlimited

OBJECTIVE: To expand vocabulary.

MATERIALS NEEDED: Dictionaries. A list of words such as: rain, game, heart, self, strong, ball, weak, water, thick, etc.

DESCRIPTION: Each student chooses one word (at a time) and tries to write as many variations of that word as he can. For example:

RAIN: rains, raining, rainy, rainproof, rainstorm, rain shower, raincheck, rainbow . . .

SUGGESTION: I usually give my students 2 minutes to think of variations, then another 3 minutes to find even more in their dictionaries. I have them draw a line after the last word they think of so they will be able to recognize and concentrate on the new ones.

95. SEVEN DEFINITIONS

L, S, R

levels: intermediate and advanced
optimal group size: 10
(For larger groups, see ADAPTATIONS.)

OBJECTIVE: To give practice in defining words. (This skill is essential in second-language communication, especially when **the** word for a concept isn't known by one of the communicants. For example: "What do you call a young dog?" and "What does 'motley' mean?"

MATERIALS NEEDED: A pile of cue cards with seven items of vocabulary on each (verbs, adjectives, nouns, prepositions, adverbs, etc.)

lunch	laugh	funny
egg	candle	dictionary
happy	fork	under
far	between	shoe
fast	heavy	wash
cry	desk	typewriter
long	eat	slowly

DESCRIPTION: Students are paired off and one partner is given a cue card. Within a time limit of 60 seconds (more or less, according to their abilities), the student must define each item on his card. His team gets one point for each item correctly identified by his partner. For example:

Student A1:	Student A2:
"It's the meal after breakfast."	"SUPPER?"
"No, between breakfast and supper."	"LUNCH?"
"Yes."	
"You eat this at breakfast."	"CEREAL?"
"No, you eat it with bacon."	"TOAST?"
"No, it comes from chickens."	"EGGS?"
"Singular!"	"EGG."
"Yes." (1 point)	

ADAPTATIONS: Divide larger groups into any number of equal teams. Each member takes a turn giving the definitions to the other members of his team.

A2		B2	
A3		B3	
A4	A1	B4	B1
A5		B5	
A6		B6	

SUGGESTIONS: I often have my students sit back-to-back to avoid the use of gestures and increase language dependency.

For less fluent students, the definitions could be written out before the game is played.

96. TRAVELOG

L, S

levels: intermediate and advanced
optimal group size: unlimited

OBJECTIVE: To review the simple past.

MATERIALS NEEDED: Slides of a trip taken by the teacher or by any of the students, and a slide projector.

DESCRIPTION: Slides of a trip are shown to the group while the students take turns contributing to a creative and imaginative oral travelog. For example:

S1: "This is where we stopped to go swimming."

S2: "Unfortunately, the water was too cold."

S3: "Then we ate at this restaurant, where the food was delicious and inexpensive."

S4: "At the zoo, we saw all kinds of animals, including this bear."

S5: "This is our motel. The beds were too soft and the walls were too thin. We could hear our neighbour's TV better than ours."

97. HINK-PINK

L, S

levels: intermediate and advanced
optimal group size: unlimited

OBJECTIVE: To develop vocabulary.

MATERIALS NEEDED: None.

DESCRIPTION: When a student thinks of a pair of one-syllable rhyming words, he says, "I have a HINK-PINK." He then gives a hint and challenges the others to discover his words. For example:

"It's a tiny sphere. What is it?"

For rhyming two-syllable words, he says, "I have a HINKY-PINKY. It's a solid piece of furniture. What is it?"

For three-syllable rhyming words: "I have a HINKETY-PINKETY. It's an evil cleric. What is it?"

Solutions for the above three examples are:

(1) SMALL BALL (2) STABLE TABLE (3) SINISTER MINISTER

The person who guesses correctly can win a point, or replace the challenger with his own challenge.

SUGGESTION: The easiest way to make up HINK-PINKS, etc, is to think of 2 rhyming words that have the same number of syllables and link them together with a definition. For example:

TALL WALL (a high divider)

or

BOOK NOOK (where you put novels)

or

BETTER SWEATER (a very good pullover)

98. BUFFET

R, W

levels: intermediate and advanced
optimal group size: unlimited

OBJECTIVE: To expand vocabulary while showing students how words are formed and the meaning of various prefixes and suffixes.

MATERIALS NEEDED: The following 3 lists of prefixes, roots and suffixes, and dictionaries.

Appetizers		Main courses	Desserts	
hyper-	in-	-dic-	-ion	-acy
mono-	im-	-dict-	-ive	-ance
a-	con-	-voc-	-ator	-ant
an-	com-	-duc-	-able	-ate
ab-	pro-	-duct-	-ible	-cy
abs-	per-	-vert-	-er	-ee
ante-	de-	-vers-	-or	-ette
anti-	pre-	-trac-	-ation	-hood
cog-	re-	-tract-	-ment	-ious
col-	ex-	-junc-	-by	-ise
com-	trans-	-junct-	-aceous	-ize
con-	poly-	-cep-	-cide	-ity
cor-	ortho-	-cept-	-ness	-tude
co-	circum-	-spec-	-rupt	-oid
extra-	hypo-	-spect-	-script	-ship
inter-	amphi-	-cred-	-ject	-ory
alter-	auto-	-jec-	-fort	-ment
anim-	bi-	-ject-	-ic	
chroma-				
chromo-				
equ-				
liber-				

DESCRIPTION: Students are given the 3 lists and compete to compile as many words as possible by combining the 3 components. For example, a student would take an appetizer, add it to a main course and attach a dessert. If the word is in the dictionary, he would write its meaning down and score one point. If the word is not in the dictionary, it is considered not to exist, and no point is won. For example:

in- + -junct- + -ion =	*A court writ whereby one is required to do or to refrain from doing a specified act.*
-dict- + -ator =	*A person ruling absolutely and often brutally and oppressively.*
anim- + -vers- + -ible =	DOES NOT EXIST

SUGGESTION: You could count 1 point per component in each acceptable word to encourage students to use the greatest number of prefixes, roots, and suffixes. If that were done, "injunction" would be worth 3 points, "dictator" would gain 2, and "animversible" zero.

99. HYBRID

L, S, R, W

levels: intermediate and advanced
optimal group size: unlimited

OBJECTIVE: To review names of some lesser known animals.

MATERIALS NEEDED: Pen and paper.

DESCRIPTION: Students are divided into groups of 4 or 5, and are challenged to create names for imaginary hybrid animals. For example:

> "Suppose a lobster mated with a termite. What would you call the baby? How about a lobsTERmite?"
>
> "How about the offspring from a kangaroo and a rooster? A kangarooster?"

Here are some other possibilities: (Keep them to yourself until the students have finished.)

mooSErpent
gorillama
hippopotaMUSkrat
elephantelope
buffaLOon
zebrattlesnake
perCHicken

cowl
fiSHrew
pelicanary
cLAMprey
turtleopard
fiSHrimp
birdonkey

SUGGESTION: I find that students grasp the idea better if they see the examples written, and the common element emphasized by capital letters or underlining.

100. PREROOTSUFF

R, W

levels: intermediate and advanced
optimal group size: 10

OBJECTIVE: To reinforce the use of prefixes and suffixes.

MATERIALS NEEDED: 101 cards per group:

25 prefixes: 10 re, 5 pre, 5 mis, 5 un

56 root words: 4 each of take, spell, tell, call, heat, view, read, cover, claim, print, fair, chill, form, and even

20 suffixes: 10 each of ed and ing

DESCRIPTION: Each player is dealt 7 cards. The rest of the cards are placed in a pile, face-down, in the centre of the table. Each player, in turn, takes the top card from the pile in the centre and discards one of his own, face-down, to the bottom of the pile. This exchange continues until one player (any player) feels confident that he has a good score and stops the game. All players then count up their scores.

Scoring: prefix + root = 10 points
root + suffix = 5 points
prefix + root + suffix = 20 points

Subtract 2 points for each unused card.

SUGGESTION: Students find it easier if prefixes are written in one colour, roots in another, and suffixes in a third colour.

101. CHARADES

S, R

levels: intermediate and advanced
optimal group size: unlimited

OBJECTIVE: To provide relaxation, reduce reticence, raise attentiveness and/or restrain restlessness.

MATERIALS NEEDED: Many phrases or short sentences written on strips of paper. Put these in a box or bag.

DESCRIPTION: Students take turns acting out what is written on the slips of paper they draw, at random, from the box. A time limit may be imposed to increase the competitive spirit of the game. For example:

> He eats pizza twice a week.
> They never go bowling on Sunday.
> My father slept on the floor last night.
> She will call him next month.

ADAPTATIONS: Larger groups (20 to 40) can be divided into teams of 5 players each. One player takes his turn acting out his CHARADE, with his team trying to guess his sentence. One team point is won if the complete sentence is guessed within the time limit. Other teams must watch quietly, or they will lose a point for distracting the actor and his team. For very advanced classes, I use familiar proverbs to be acted out (for example, "You can lead a horse to water, but you can't make him drink.")

SUGGESTION: Before the game is played, I always establish gestures for: "Number of words" (such as displaying the corresponding number of fingers while touching the outside of a bent elbow); "First word," "Second word," "Number of syllables" (corresponding number of fingers displayed on the inside of a straight elbow); "Sounds like" (pulling at the earlobe); "Opposite" (making an upside-down gesture as though one were holding an object with two hands); "Same as" (meshing the fingers of both hands); "Past" (gesturing back, over the shoulder); "Present" (pointing down in front of you); "Future" (pointing ahead of you); and any other generally helpful symbols that come to mind before, during, or after the game.

102. WONDER WORD

R, W

levels: intermediate and advanced
optimal group size: unlimited

OBJECTIVE: To expand vocabulary.

MATERIALS NEEDED: Several WONDER WORDS on paper, overhead, or blackboard.

DESCRIPTION: Students are presented with several WONDER WORDS and are challenged to find the common word. For example:

1.	2.
________ garden	________ drop
________ bush	________ fall
red ________	________ coat
________ bud	________ storm
________ mary	________ shower
________ water	acid ________

3.	4.
butter ___________	___________ dew
___________ swatter	___________ comb
___________ paper	___________ moon
___________ wheel	___________ suckle
___________ fishing	___________ bee

SUGGESTION: To aid students, dashes could be used to represent the letters of the missing WONDER WORD. For example:

_ _ _ _ garden, _ _ _ _ drop, butter _ _ _, etc.

Here are a few more to help get you started:

station wagon, newspaper, waterfall, car wash, sidewalk

103. SABERED STORIES

R, L, S

levels: intermediate and advanced
optimal group size: unlimited

OBJECTIVE: To increase comprehension and appreciation of sequence.

MATERIALS NEEDED: Segments of a short story written on individual index cards (5 to 10 cards per story). For example:

> /Joe's friend, Bob, loved money very much./
>
> /So much, in fact, that he never gave any to anyone./
>
> /One day, Joe, Bob, and a couple of other friends were walking near the river, when Bob suddenly fell in./
>
> /One of the others reached out for him and said, "Give me your hand and I'll pull you out!" but Bob just kept splashing around and crying for help./

/Another friend came to the edge of the water and yelled, "Give me your hand and I'll save you!" but Bob went down yet another time, without reaching for his friend's hand./

/Then Joe said, "Take my hand!" and Bob stretched out his hand and was pulled to safety./

/The others were amazed and confused./

/Joe explained: "You don't know Bob like I do."/

/"When you say 'GIVE' to him, he does nothing."/

/"But when you say 'TAKE', he takes."/

DESCRIPTION: Each student is given 1 card and is responsible for that card. Together, the group must decide on the order in which the cards must be arranged to make a logical, interesting story.

SUGGESTIONS: I divide classes of 30 to 40 students into 4 to 5 groups and give each group a SABERED STORY.

I don't allow students to look at one another's cards. Each student reads his card to the group as often as is necessary to determine the proper sequence.

104. ENCYCLOPEDIA

L, S

level: advanced
optimal group size: unlimited

OBJECTIVE: To develop critical listening skills.

MATERIALS NEEDED: A set of encyclopedia.

DESCRIPTION: The class is divided into 5 teams. The teacher reads the descriptive account of a famous person or a familiar place, while the students try to guess the identity of the person or place being described. Students are allowed to interrupt the reading to guess.

Scoring: Minus 2 points for each wrong guess. (This reduces wild guessing.)
Plus 5 for a correct guess.

Team members are permitted to confer with one another during the game.

105. LIFEBOAT

L, S

level: advanced
optimal group size: 10

OBJECTIVE: To spark controversy and stimulate conversation.

MATERIALS NEEDED: The names of 12 famous people, or 12 professions, on slips of paper which are put into a bag.

DESCRIPTION: Each student chooses (randomly) the name of a profession or a famous person. They all imagine that they are survivors of a shipwreck whose lifeboat is sure to sink, unless one of them jumps overboard and sacrifices his life for the sake of the others. Then, each one in turn must try to convince the others of his value to the group, and to society in general, in order to save himself. When all have spoken, each one votes for the person he feels should jump out, and explains his reasons to the rest of the group.

ADAPTATION: This game has also been known as Balloon (of the hot-air variety) and Bomb Shelter, but it is played exactly the same way.

Occasionally, instead of having names of famous people written on the slips, I write a short biographical note on each. In this way, the relative popularity of the celebrity doesn't affect the voting. For example:

> You are a sixty-eight-year-old doctor, in good mental and physical health.
>
> You are a twenty-one-year-old rock singer.
>
> You are a twenty-three-year-old straight-A student of urban architecture.
>
> You are the pregnant mother of 4 young children.
>
> You are an important government official.

106. HOMONYMS

R, L, S

level: advanced
optimal group size: 10

OBJECTIVE: To familiarize students with various homonyms.

MATERIALS NEEDED: Cards with a pair (or more) of homonyms on each.

DESCRIPTION: Each student takes one card from the inverted pile and uses the homonyms in oral sentences. One point for each correct sentence. For example:

HEAR HERE	I **hear** a bird singing. My book is **here**, yours is there.
THERE THEIR THEY'RE	**There** is a blue Ford. **Their** car is green. **They're** going to the movies tonight.

Here's a partial list of common homonyms to get you started: road/rode; waist/waste; red/read; to/too/two; chord/cored/cord; reed/read; bear/bare; way/weigh; week/weak; beet/beat; missed/mist; sent/scent/cent; sale/sail; dear/deer; seen/scene; loan/lone; some/sum; I/eye/(aye); seem/seam; wait/weight; hair/hare; flower/flour; steak/stake; see/sea; our/hour; piece/peace; so/sew; meat/meet; led/lead; principal/principle; wood/would; one/won; pair/pare/pear; son/sun; bye/buy/by; mail/male . . .

SUGGESTIONS: Occasionally, a student has difficulty creating a sentence which shows the meaning of a word even though he knows what it means. When this happens, I award a point for a good definition of the word. Other students learn new words when homonyms are spelled.

107. RHYME

R, W

level: advanced
optimal group size: unlimited

OBJECTIVE: To have some fun writing short poems.

MATERIALS NEEDED: Pen and paper for each student.

DESCRIPTION: Each student writes 4 words on his paper. The first and third, second and fourth, must rhyme. The students then pair off, exchange papers, and try to write a short poem using each other's words. For example, the words might be: *sleep, clock, deep* and *dock.*

Someone might come up with the following poem:

> When I go to **sleep,**
> I hear the **clock.**
> But when I sleep **deep,**
> I hope I'm not on a **dock.**

108. DETAILED INSTRUCTIONS

L, S, R, W

level: advanced
optimal group size: unlimited

OBJECTIVE: To give students practice in giving and receiving precise instructions.

MATERIALS NEEDED: Pen and paper for each student.

DESCRIPTION: Each student chooses a task to explain and writes a **detailed** description of the actions to be performed. He then chooses a partner and reads his instructions to his partner who, in turn, follows each instruction **explicitly**. For example:

How to –
- tie a shoelace
- eat spaghetti
- put on and button a shirt
- change a flat tire
- sharpen a pencil
- put on and do up a belt
- brush your teeth
- cut and eat a steak
- change the oil in a car
- fix a bicycle tire
- take a picture with a camera (35 mmSLR)

SUGGESTIONS: To encourage my students to be exact, I tell them to pretend that they are going to describe how to do something to someone who has never done it before. For example: "You are going to tell someone how to tie a shoelace. He has never seen nor worn shoes before in his life." To discourage the use of gestures, they could sit back to back.

109. WHAT'S NEW?

L, S, R, W

level: advanced
optimal group size: unlimited

OBJECTIVE: To refine listening skills.

MATERIALS NEEDED: A tape recorder, a taped newscast, dictionaries, and a list of questions about the newscast.

DESCRIPTION: The class is divided into 2 teams. A newscast is played for the group while they take notes, as required. At the end of the newscast, the teacher poses questions, alternately, to members of each team. Two points are earned for each correct response. If a member of one team cannot answer correctly and fully, a member of the other team can gain 1 point by giving the correct answer. Questions should cover many listening skills, such as: listening for details; to note general significance; to draw conclusions; to determine the accuracy of statements; to get the sequence of events; to identify known personalities mentioned; to form opinions; to determine reasons behind events; to speculate on future developments; and to gain an appreciation of past events and how they have affected other incidents.

SUGGESTIONS: For Canadian schools, I recommend using CBC newscasts since they are the most complete and in-depth of any coverage I have heard. For those within range of CJRT-FM (basically anywhere in Ontario with cable), there is a BBC newscast at 8 a.m. Monday - Saturday, which concentrates on international news and issues with which some of your students may be familiar. Before presenting the newscast, I always write unfamiliar vocabulary on the board. This enables us to familiarize ourselves with new words before hearing them in context.

110. RELATIVELY SPEAKING

R, W

level: advanced
optimal group size: unlimited

OBJECTIVE: To review various idiomatic expressions.

MATERIALS NEEDED: The following examples on the blackboard or overhead.

1. $\frac{\text{stand}}{\text{i}}$

2. ter/very/esting

DESCRIPTION: The teacher shows the above examples to the class and asks them what they think the coded puzzles mean. Students eventually discover that the first example means "I understand," and the second means "very interesting." Several other examples can now be presented and the students are challenged to decipher them. For example:

b/sick/ed (sick in bed)

```
        s
      t
    s
  o
c
```

(rising costs)

```
    r
    o
r o a d s
    d
    s
```

(crossroads)

$\frac{\text{area}}{\text{populated}}$ (overpopulated area)

When the class has found the solutions to the above examples, students can work in pairs to create their own graphic depictions of known idiomatic expressions.

Here are some that my students have conceived:

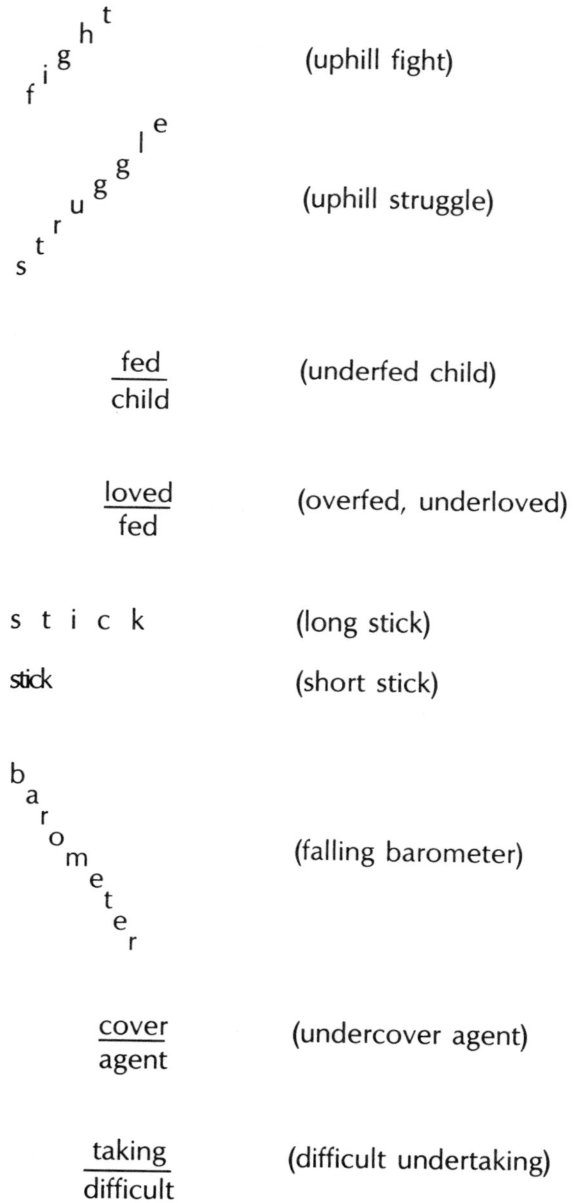

GAINS (capital gains)

sur/fire/ance (fire insurance)

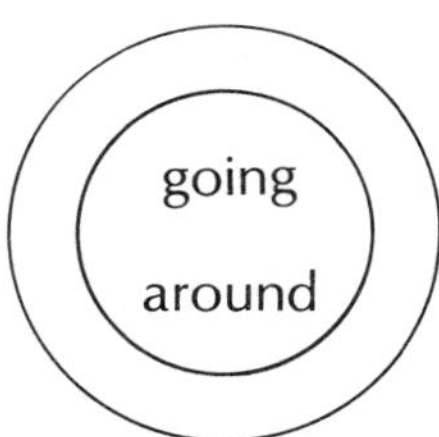

(going around in circles)

his iiii
OO (dark circles under his eyes)

ar/up/ms (up in arms)

I'm
time (I'm on time)

working
time (working overtime)

p – a – n – t – s (stretch pants)

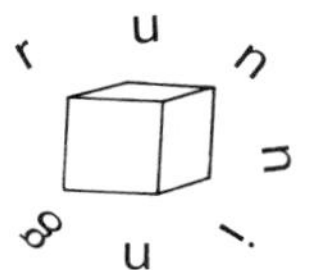

(running around the block)

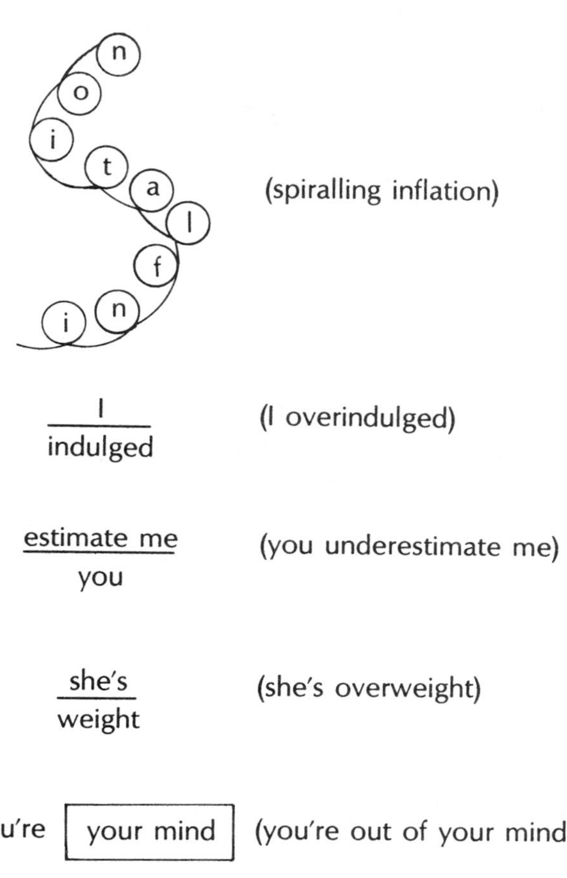

(spiralling inflation)

I / indulged — (I overindulged)

estimate me / you — (you underestimate me)

she's / weight — (she's overweight)

you're [your mind] — (you're out of your mind)

wear / clean — (clean underwear)

INDEX

(Numbers refer to GAME NUMBER, not page number.)

W.

Y.

ABOUT THE AUTHOR

Jerry Steinberg attended the University of Toronto and McMaster University, receiving his degree in Linguistics and French from the University of Guelph after graduating from Hamilton Teachers' College, where he had specialized in teaching French as a Second Language.

He has taught English and French as Second Languages to children and adults in Ontario, Quebec and British Columbia since 1968.

In addition to his duties at Columbia College in Burnaby, B.C., he conducts workshops based on his book, *Games Language People Play,* with language professionals throughout Canada and the United States on a free-lance basis. He also presents workshops on using comics to teach languages, entitled *Wha'cha Gonna Learn From Comics?*, which will soon appear under the Pippin Publishing/Dominie Press imprint.

He is the volunteer Executive Director of AIRSPACE Non-smokers' Rights Society in Vancouver, and is also the founder of a social group for couples and singles who don't have children. The group is called NO KIDDING!.

He lives with his wife, cat and three dogs in South Surrey, British Columbia.